JOURNEY BY FAITH

*Discovering and Fulfilling
the Will of God: NOW!*

By William Owens

Journey By Faith
Discovering and Fulfilling the Will of God: NOW!

Copyright   2002 1 by William Owens
william@journeybyfaith.net

Published by:
Through People, LLC
www.throughpeople.com

Owens, William, 1964
Discovering and Fulfilling the Will of God: NOW!

p. cm.
ISBN: 978-1-68524-803-1
1. Owens, William 1964 2. Clergy
1st Printing 2021

All scripture quotations are taken from the Holy Bible King James Version.

All rights reserved. No part of this publication may be reproduced, stored in a retrieval system, or transmitted in any form or by any means-electronic, mechanical, photocopy, recording, or any other except for brief quotations in printed reviews, without the written permission of the publisher.

Cover Design Concept: Xee_designs1
Printed in the United States of America

TABLE OF CONTENTS

Introduction — 7
Why God Had Me To Write This Book.. *11*

CHAPTER ONE
The Journey Within — 15
Meet for the Master's Use... *18*
Journey Into The Heart Of God... *26*

CHAPTER TWO
Identifying Your Origin of Faith — 35
Faith During the Time of Grace... *44*
How to identify your origin of faith... *49*
The Drudgery of Church Life.. *53*

CHAPTER THREE
Your Journey Starts With a Step of Faith — 57
It's not an option because we don't need one..................................... *64*
How to Initiate Your Faith.. *67*
Your Own Righteousness.. *69*
Obedience that works by Faith... *72*
Who is Your King Agag.. *79*
What is your bleating sheep?.. *81*
Obedience Because of Love.. *84*
Suffering.. *91*
Marriage and Faith.. *98*
Being Single... *100*
Single Men.. *101*
Single Women... *103*

CHAPTER FOUR
Discovering the Will of God — 107
I follow after... *108*
Forgetting Those Things... *109*
Press Toward the Mark... *111*
Be Thus Minded.. *112*
The Evidence... *116*
Your adversary, the devil.. *118*

Be Filled with All the Fulness of God and Go Forth! *119*
Your Body – The vessel for the Will of God *121*

CHPATER FIVE
The Kingdom of God — 127
Where to Pray *129*
My Father *131*
Hallowed be thy Name *131*
Thy Kingdom Come *134*
Who alone, but Jesus, made this clear? *136*
Thy Will Be Done *137*
What Happens Next *140*
Give us this day our daily bread *143*
For thine is the kingdom *144*
What Is Perfection? *155*
Your Walk Matters *158*
Keeping your body under *160*
Distractions *163*
A good conscience towards God *165*

CHAPTER SIX
Rewards and Loss — 169
This Journey is Eternal *169*
Let us be ever mindful that God is a rewarder! *176*

CHAPTER SEVEN
Dead Faith — 181
Faith, if it hath not works, is dead being alone *183*
I will shew thee my faith by my works *184*
The devils also believe *186*
Your Journey is God's Choice *189*
Examples of Faith *189*
A Prestitute Cuts a Deal *192*

CHAPTER EIGHT
Jesus Will Complete the Work — 195
He Is Our Confidence *198*
So what do you do? *199*

BONUS MATERIAL
Steps to Rebuild Your Faith — 200

POETIC
EXPRESSIONS

1045

INTRODUCTION

For the last five years, I have embarked upon the most intense, lonely, exhilarating, passionate, revealing, rewarding, painful, and purposed-filled journey of my life! I have slept in my suburban for a year, rode my bike over 1,000 miles in sharing the gospel of Jesus Christ, travel by RV for 2-years only to do it faster, written over 1,500 poems, and there is so much more. God also blessed me to produce my first poetry concert on DVD entitled, Poetic Expressions of Hope, Love, and Forgiveness. A 2-hour video production that blew my mind at what God can and will do when you take Him at His word and jump into the journey He has called you to fulfill.

If there was ever a time for you as a human being to discover your journey and to take it by faith, that time is right NOW! The return of Christ couldn't be closer, and if you intend to experience the rewards He has for you, you will only obtain them as you take your JOURNEY BY FAITH!

Never in the history of the world has there been such an overwhelming availability of God's eternal Word. With countless Bible universities, online courses, and Bible teachings that span the globe, there are zero excuses for not, in some form or fashion, hearing God's Word and coming into a degree of knowledge of what He requires of each of us. Our conscience knows the difference between good and evil unless we have rejected truth to such a degree that we have become reprobates and have been given over to delusion to believe the lie.

Bible prophecies, apologetics, history, and current events collide with vivid accuracy to provide extraordinary evidence that the Bible is legitimate, which means it is all accurate or not true at all. It is God-inspired, or the greatest hoax ever devised by man. Even so, with the highest level of intelligence, one yet cannot see this truth with the sheer wisdom of men. Though there are centuries of validation and even more recent discoveries in just the last decade of the Bible's validity, unless the eyes of the heart are opened by divine intervention, eternal truths remain foolish to the World's learned and wise.

If you scoff at the authority of scripture and the demands of a Holy God, this book is not for you in the scene; it will edify your strife to obtain and fulfill God's Will. I can only pray that you will be granted grace to confront and consider the truth of one thing: You were made with and for purpose. Even the religious will have a more difficult time with these truths because the traditions and commandments of men make the Word of God of no effect (Mark 7:13).

In any event, to continue on a path of potential eternal separation from He Who is Love, Light, and Redemption is a travesty of eternal dividends for any soul. The truth of gnashing of teeth and eternal fire will come to bear to everyone who has rejected the love of God by refusing to accept Jesus Christ as the ONLY way, the ONLY truth, and the ONLY life with evidence of obedience to His Word and the doing of His Will.

For those who embrace truth and have accepted the authority of the Word of God by humbling themselves to the ONE it has declared to be the redeemer of their souls – JESUS, I know this book will speak to their spirits as you discover that God has a will for them, and they can fulfill it by FAITH!

In this book, by the divine strength of God's grace, and revelation by the impartation of the Holy Spirit, with the authority of the scriptures, I make plain the power of faith to discover with certainty and to fulfill completely every aspect of God's Will and to do so NOW!

I will only write of what I know, and what I have lived. Through my own personal testimonies, I will validate how faith has allowed me to experience the presence of God, the provision of God, and the power of God operating in my life to do exploits for Him as I store up for myself treasures for life to come. I also humbly admit that this same grace has allowed me to deal with my failures, shortcomings and made it vividly, and at times painfully clear, that I can do nothing without Jesus. Absolutely nothing!

As part of this introduction, you must empty yourself of religious thinking. For some, that will not only be difficult but others simply impossible. You might think that saying "impossible" is inappropriate because "with God," nothing shall be impossible. Well, this is precisely my point. It must be "WITH" God. Many of God's people have replaced God with the traditions of men and have therefore made the WORD of God of none effect as referenced earlier. Though many such are truly "saved" and have accepted the atonement found in Jesus, they have yet become a pawn of religion, the religious system, and the commandments of men. Others are simply "bastards".

(Hebrews 12:8) KJV
[8] "But if ye be without chastisement, whereof all are partakers, then are ye bastards, and not sons."

They are void of any fruit and have rejected the correction in which all of God's children are partakers. Such are children of the devil! They wrestle the scriptures to their own destruction (2 Peter 3:16). They are whited sepulchers, and it would have been better for them to have not known the way of righteousness than to know it and turn the grace of God into lasciviousness (2 Peter 2:21; Jude 1:4). I'll address this in more depth in one of the chapters because I believe the devil has his ministers who have one primary assignment: to keep you from an obedient faith. Faith that does not obey God's will is nothing more than an empty hope and a dead religion.

Why God Had Me To Write This Book

God has pressed upon me to write this book for precise reasons and do so with an immense sense of urgency. Therefore, I encourage you to not take this book of instruction lightly, in a passive mindset, or just to be spiritually entertained. If that is your mindset, it would be wise to give it away, lay it down, or avoid it altogether because both you and I will be held accountable for knowing these truths. If we neglect them, there will be consequences. Though I'm not necessarily referring to the consequence of eternal separation from God as an unbeliever, I am clearly referring to the possibility of the eternal loss of reward as a believer.

(1 Corinthians 3:14-15)
KJV [14] "If any man's work abide which he hath built thereupon, he shall receive a reward. [15] If any man's work shall be burned, he shall suffer loss: but he himself shall be saved; yet so as by fire."

1. Time is of the essence - God is preparing to end the dispensation of grace, and the time to accomplish that which He has shown you is about to end. He is saying, "Get it done, NOW!"

2. You know enough! So many of God's people have gotten stuck in preparation. Years of study, working, planning, and acquiring resources have only prolonged the actual doing of His Will. These entrapments have been nothing but a distraction and will not bring you close to actually "DOING" His Will. Take what He has given you and start. It is in taking the journey by faith that will teach you more than any classroom could.

3. Confronting Your Carnal Lifestyle. Despite the upheaval of life as we know it in the world, the declining economy, the increase of immorality, and the spiritual weakness that is apparent in most churches, many of God's people are still trying to maintain a level of lifestyle that is centered on the love of the world. They do so by holding on to the elusive "American Dream", which has long eroded. What was once the norm is being replaced daily with a more evil and sinister agenda. We should rejoice because it is a sign of the times. We choose to either resolve this hindrance by self-denial or wait until we found ourselves overwhelmed with the fallout when it does happen. By adapting, you can move on to maturity and begin to DO God's Will – NOW!

4. Lastly, Arise to the Battle – God wants you to know that HE is the ONLY source you need to discover and fulfill His Will. He wants you to fully embrace HIM and what He has told you to do. He wants you to rely on Him for everything in your life. He wants you to experience Him every second of every minute of every hour, of every day, of every week, of every month, of every year, of every decade, of your entire existence now and throughout eternity! All you need is faith in Him!

I ask that you prayerfully read this book with a repentant heart. When you are convicted, that simply means repent to God and ask Him to wash you with His Word and then move away from that act or mindset by shifting to obedience through faith.

At the writing of this book, I am also teaching a series on this very topic at www.journeybyfaith.net . You can enroll for the entire lesson and download the workbook to go along with this teaching. It is time to begin.

Fearless,

William A. Owens

Evangelist William Owens
March 2021
Mobile, AL

Chapter One

THE JOURNEY WITHIN

Every Journey Starts Within the Heart

(John 1:4) KJV

[4] *"In him was life; and the life was the light of men."*

"Let's Go!"
"Just Do It!"
"If you can believe it, you can achieve it!"

These are just a few of the mantras that are well known to us. They reflect the self-determined heart to do what it wants to do because it can do it. Regardless of who we are, we deceive ourselves into thinking the inside will arrive if we become that person on the outside. It never works out that way.

God's heart is broken when He looks at His people in the USA because we have adopted the ways of the world. We have patterned our methods to pursue the "vision", to accomplish some great work or become a great minister, an artist, speaker, athlete, actor, and tag, "Jesus is Lord" behind it. Yet, all along, deep inside, our journey is stagnant, stale, and predictable. The journey inside isn't moving. We avoided that journey altogether by dressing up the outside, making plans, and gathering around us the same kind of people, so in a real journey, people do not threaten us.

Before God takes you to a physical place of destiny and purpose, He's going to take you to an inward place of discovery. Before God exalts you before men, He wants you to humble yourself before Him. He wants to know you for Himself. He wants you to discover Who He is for yourself. It is about intimacy. Spirit to spirit. Heart to heart. Discovery of who God is and, therefore, who you are. It is becoming acquainted with your eternal Heavenly Father, Jesus your Savior, and the Holy Spirit, your guide. To reject this journey is to abandon your salvation because they are the same. If we have accepted the atoning work of Christ, we did so to become sons of God willingly and, therefore, to submit ourselves to His Will and the Lordship of Christ. They then take residence within us and make their abode in us.

(John 14:23) KJV
"Jesus answered and said unto him, If a man love me, he will keep my words: and my Father will love him, and we will come unto him, and make our abode with him."

This foundation of intimacy is what the journey is all about. It begins within your heart. Nothing will, and no one can live within you, but God and His only begotten Son, Jesus. He is that light. It is Christ within you that all the issues of life exist. It is where the kingdom begins, ends, and then begins again. It is where the lover of your soul meets you and heals you to bring you more into Himself and therefore more into the eternal person, He made you be. It is not about the life you see, the flesh you handle, society, and the temporal realm of existence that illicit your soul and passions to bondage. All these things are passing away - even now. He is preparing an eternal rule that will never end, and only on the inside of you can He prepare you to rule with Him – now and in the life to come.

(John 15:4-8) KJV
"Abide in me, and I in you. As the branch cannot bear fruit of itself, except it abide in the vine; no more can ye, except ye abide in me. [5] I am the vine, ye are the branches: He that abideth in me, and I in him, the same bringeth forth much fruit: for without me ye can do nothing. [6] If a man abide not in me, he is cast forth as a branch, and is withered; and men gather them, and cast them into the fire, and they are burned. [7] If ye abide in me, and my words abide in you, ye shall ask what ye will, and it shall be done unto you. [8] Herein is my Father glorified, that ye bear much fruit; so shall ye be my disciples."

Abiding in Christ is all about an inward journey. It testifies that this is where God begins and, therefore, where we must also begin. All the self-determined efforts are futile and meaningless to our Holy God! The works of the flesh are repulsive to Him, and He does not need our works. He wants the heart! He wants to dwell on the inside of the most sacred place of who you are. He wants to abide in you and is inviting you to take a journey within. In this, He is glorified in the spiritual fruit you will bear by His Spirit. You will then be found a vessel meet for the Master's use.

MEET FOR THE MASTER'S USE

(2 Timothy 2:19-21) KJV
"Nevertheless the foundation of God standeth sure, having this seal, The Lord knoweth them that are his. And, Let every one that nameth the name of Christ depart from iniquity. [20] But in a great house there are not only vessels of gold and of silver, but also of wood and of earth; and some to honour, and some to dishonour. [21] If a man therefore purge himself from these, he shall be a vessel unto honour, sanctified, and meet for the master's use, and prepared unto every good work."

Is it strange to fully accept that the Lord knows them that are His? This knowing is not passive or of a religious kick. It is more profound than that of sex, food, success, and all the pleasures of the world that can be tasted, touched, and touted! Being known of God starts with Him inviting you for you to invite Him into your heart, into your being, and into the very seat of your soul. When you do, you willingly do so. God has never made anyone worship Him. If He did, it would not be worship. Even the angles have the liberty to serve Him. If not, how could Lucifer have deceived a third of them? Under the law and the dispensation of grace, God has never forced a living soul, ever created, to bow one knee to Him[1]. That includes Satan. However, the day will come that every knee shall bow.

The journey God has for each of us has a standard that is indeed the same. They are required and necessary because they represent His character and the far-reaching mysterious will that we cannot understand to any degree. He's more interested in preparing us for an eternal reign than anything that we do for Him in this life. Though our labors in this life will reflect the rewards that we receive, any work is only as good as the relationship that they were borne from. We should avoid the traps, which can also void our labors because we reject God from being God within us. We must "strive lawfully" if we are to be crowned.

(2 Timothy 2:5) KJV
"And if a man also strive for masteries, yet is he not crowned, except he strive lawfully."

- **Departing from iniquity** – An authentic journey with God cannot include habitual sin, bondage to sin,

---

[1] Though one day every knee shall bow, and every tongue confess that Jesus is Lord, that day has not yet come. Once the dispensation of grace has ended and we transition into judgement, all invitations are off the table.

or weakness in areas of your life that involve the cycle of sin. Be assured that there is a loophole for those who want it to justify sin in their lives.

- The bottom line is that the inward journey involves the purification of your vessel. Though this is an ongoing process, but you know when you are "on par" with God. In other words, you are walking where you have attained and have a clear conscience with Him in every area of your life. You have a mindset to obey God and are not a slave to sin. Your body is under control, and your heart is sensitive to the Holy Spirit and will not grieve Him. When you suffer in the flesh, you cease from sin because your heart is to please God (1 Peter 4:1). Until you allow the power of His resurrection to work in you, your journey will remain in this place until you yield to the freedom that Christ has secured for you.

- Vessels of Honor and Dishonor – God has placed within you vessels of honor that you will not know fully in this life. The journey within is to discover them. You must unearth the gold, the silver, the precious gems, and to do so; you must rid yourselves of the wood and the earth. God does not do this for you but has given you that same power that rose Jesus from the dead to do so. He will not use the vessels of the sensual to fulfill His Will in you. Many Christians have subject themselves to fleshly efforts and work to please God, thinking that their gifts will manifest

His glory within them. It will not. Let's be reminded of those who did many wonderful works, but Jesus never "knew" them.

- Purge yourself – After you pray for deliverance, you put away the sin, idols, and carnal habits. God has done His part in spiritually setting you free and breaking the power of the devil off your life and translating you into the Kingdom of His dear Son. What more do you want? A relationship is in two ways. He has given, and we now receive by yielding ourselves to righteousness. The degree you align yourself with His likeness, His holiness, His ways within your spirit and through your body will reflect in the presence manifested in work He does through you. The emphasis is on HIS presence manifested – not the work in and of itself.

- Meet for the Master's use and prepared unto every good work – What thrills God is not always what thrills us. Yet, when we trust His ways and take this journey within, we come to experience an inward joy that is not determined by the work we do but rather by the God we know. It will only be through this kingdom standard that He is using us will become an outward journey that will manifest into 'every good work'. What's more important to God is that we come to learn, regardless of how He uses us that our communion with Him is the foundation of our journey, and it will never be replaced by the 'good work' that we do.

While there are many other biblical standards that both establish and propel our journey by faith, I believe the above principles open the gateway to understanding the non-negotiable requirement of the inward journey with God. It is where the outward journey is discovered and fulfilled. I am persuaded that we avoid, knowingly or not, this inward journey because many within the Body of Christ have been led to believe that believing God is doing the things of God, but not God, Himself. We have erected idols of many kinds that only serve the religious order and make many rich in the process. One example of this is worship.

Worship within Christianity today, for many, has become an idol. From famous artists, concerts, and conferences; worshipping has become a consuming part of who we are. The object of worship has become a god who understands us, comforts us, and tolerates us. He is doing His job in pleasing us regardless of how we live our inward lives. If one has enough discernment to see it, minimal emphasis, if at all, in today's worship, is on God Himself. It is rather on ourselves. Discern the idea:

- You know my heart
- Heal my pain
- Bring me home
- Deliver me, again
- My trouble
- Forgive me
- I know you're there no matter what
- I'm sorry
- I apologize
- Mercy

Now please, don't get me wrong. There is a time for these songs, and I'm not suggesting they are irrelevant. These songs bring great comfort and are needed during seasons in our lives. However, when we choose to live there and use these characteristics of God to refuse God what He wants – our hearts; it's not the repeat of the same lyrics but a new song that springs forth from a new journey every day.

Consider Lucifer. He was created to worship. However, his worship became the center of his purpose and not WHO he was made to honor. It was then that he looked within himself and took pleasure in his voice, in his words, in his beauty and iniquity was found in him. I don't believe this happened in 30 days. It took considerable time for this subtle temptation to take root, germinate, and then spread within his mind to finally bring forth a full-blown rejection of God and the foolish idea that he could exalt his throne above God. He even forgot that he didn't have a throne. Lucifer talks about sin making you guilty and stupid.

    I am pointing out worship because it appeals to the flesh in various ways and can be persuaded to substitute a genuine relationship with God. It does this by allowing the soul to worship itself. It is why so many people who lead worship become captive to carnal and fleshly tendencies. Worship without the inward journey being established will lure the flesh to the flesh, and it causes people to follow the same pitfall of Lucifer. He persuaded the angels to worship him. When he recognized the effect that he had on the angels, it had a role in him being convinced that he could usurp God. It is why the journey within the heart is so important. It establishes a strong bond with God and secures a bond of love that will compromise for anything or anyone. It is why Jesus was able to carry forth His ministry amid total rejection of men and even His disciples when brought before Pilate. He did not seek the glory of men, nor did He want it because He knew what was in man.

(John 2 25) KJV
"And needed not that any should testify of man: for he knew what was in man."

Consider the real temptation Satan offered Him?

(Matthew 4:9) KJV
"And saith unto him, All these things will I give thee, if thou wilt fall down and worship me."

I know we think of this temptation as perhaps a nonchalant challenge to Jesus; after all, He is the Son of God. That is a false assumption. Remember, Jesus was also fully man. He, therefore, felt the appeal of the flesh. Jesus could avoid this horrendous crucifixion and bow a knee to Satan and settle for the kingdoms of this world. He rejected this and reinforced the truth.

(Matthew 4:10) KJV
"Then saith Jesus unto him, Get thee hence, Satan: for it is written, Thou shalt worship the Lord thy God, and him only shalt thou serve."

You see, this is why worship is dangerous outside the inward journey of the heart between you and God. When we embrace the inward journey, God exposes the idols, the pain, the issues, the filth, and the curses that we are under, the bondage, the anger, the unforgiveness, and unclean places that provide habitation for darkness. It is the private journey of building up your new man in spirit and truth. It is a season of the Son making you free indeed, and you become acquainted with the Father's voice, His ways with you, and out of this beauty, glimmers of His Will begin to manifest. The good work He has called you to speak to you with such clarity, and the presence of His grace is tangibly manifested to you.

The inward journey by faith is awaiting you every morning and is anticipating your presence throughout the day, especially as you prepare to rest for the night. This inward journey is ever-increasing, and you'll discover therein is revealed every journey God has intended for you to experience in this life and in the life to come. Don't think of your journey as doing something; your journey is into God Himself, and out of Him, you become. In becoming, you do by His Spirit the work He has done in you. The blessedness of this inward journey brings us into a discovery of the origin of our faith. The revelation of Him knowing us before He formed us and the reason He sanctified and ordained us before He brought us forth from our mothers' womb. It also makes our fruit possible to remain and ensure when the fire tries our works, they endure.

JOURNEY INTO THE HEART OF GOD

The ultimate of all ultimate's is discovering the Heart of God for yourself. It must be a program that includes music by a famous artist, a sermon by a popular preacher, and a personal prophecy would be fantastic! I shouldn't have to say, "for yourself"; however, so much in Christianity has become a movement or an event that I believe most people feel like they can only discover the heart of God through something or someone other than Jesus.

None of these can take you into the heart of God. They can serve to prepare you or put you in a proper spiritual position should they be done in spirit and truth. However, the journey into the Heart of God is hidden and must be discovered by you alone. It is a mysterious union of Creator and creation in which the Creator creates a desire within His creation to want to know Him for Him alone. I will be redundant a bit because we tend to hear or read with preconceived ideas that hold us into a traditional mindset, and we miss the truth of what is being said. For example, we can equate seeking God with going to church, studying the Bible, serving in a particular ministry, or office, leading worship, and even "getting saved." Discovering the Heart of God is none of these no more than discovering your husband or wife is merely having dinner together, holding hands, or having an intimate evening together. Seeking God and loving your spouse is essential. Yet, discovering a person is beyond the activity we do with that person.

God wants nothing more than for you to discover His Heart. His heart is filled with mystery rooted in an eternal love in which He wants to be loved for Who He is. God is love and seeks to be loved from a heart that has received His love and desires to give this love back to Him for Him alone. He wants to be loved by your heart like you love no one else. Not because He can do for you, but because He is everything you need and desire. I didn't say, He can "give" you everything you need and want. I said He "is" everything you need and desire.

We are so controlled by the elements of creation that we can't imagine life without anything but God Himself. We, therefore, associate God with ideas, a denomination, a song, a sermon, church attendance, and a host of other created expressions that we pay homage to while thinking they are God. They are NOT God. God is God, and to discover His Heart, you must go to Him and Him only through Jesus Christ, who has shown us the way. He is the way, the truth, and the life, and no one comes to the Father but by Him.

So, what does discovering the Heart of God look like? I can't tell you that because the Heart of God is different for each of us. No man can even teach you to know the Lord, no more than a man can teach a man or woman to love their wife or husband. It is intimate.

(Hebrews 8; 11) KJV
"And they shall not teach every man his neighbour, and every man his brother, saying, Know the Lord: for all shall know me, from the least to the greatest."

I can assure you that it can only begin when you are exhausted from discovering everything and everyone else. Even then, God must draw you to the secret place of His heart.

(Psalm 65:4) KJV
"Blessed is the man whom thou choosest, and causest to approach unto thee, that he may dwell in thy courts: we shall be satisfied with the goodness of thy house, even of thy holy temple."

(Psalm 91:1-2) KJV
"He that dwelleth in the secret place of the most High shall abide under the shadow of the Almighty. [2] I will say of the LORD, He is my refuge and my fortress: my God; in him will I trust."

Loving the Lord your God with all your heart, mind, soul, and strength is the greatest commandment and the sole essence of your journey. It is on this basis that your journey by faith must reside. Any other motive will fall short, and you will wander in a wilderness of cycles that are designed to bring you to this truth: God wants you to discover His Heart. When you do, you will find everything that pertains to who you are. That is because He made you.

(Jeremiah 1-5) KJV
"Before I formed thee in the belly I knew thee; and before thou camest forth out of the womb I sanctified thee, and I ordained thee a prophet unto the nations."

As you take on the Journey by Faith, an attitude of childlike faith will make your journey simple. Any other attitude will complicate this spiritual experience. When Jesus said it, He meant it because He understands our nature is to want to know every detail before we do anything. The bottom line is we want to control, but the journey is all about giving up control.

(Matthew 18:2-4) KJV
"And Jesus called a little child unto him, and set him in the midst of them, [3] And said, Verily I say unto you, Except ye be converted, and become as little children, ye shall not enter into the kingdom of heaven. [4] Whosoever therefore shall humble himself as this little child, the same is greatest in the kingdom of heaven."

Begin your journey into the Heart of God with silence and stillness. It is a show of humility and reverence. In today's church culture, we have lost that. Each of us needs to reset our awareness of Who God Is. We need to forget what we know and start afresh, allowing God to show us Himself for that to happen.

(Hebrews 12:28-29) KJV
"Wherefore we receiving a kingdom which cannot be moved, let us have grace, whereby we may serve God acceptably with reverence and godly fear: [29] For our God is a consuming fire."

(Daniel 10:15) KJV
"And when he had spoken such words unto me, I set my face toward the ground, and I became dumb."

Make yourself venerable. Make yourself humble. Make yourself as one that is dumb (speechless). When you do speak, let it come from the depth of your heart. Prepare to spend devoted and extended time before God. You are mistaken if you think you can take a journey to discover God's Heart with few minutes here and there to spare. Time is of no essence because He rules over time, and you are in a space that desiring God has become your passion for He has created this hunger in you.

Relating to God requires becoming acquainted with His character, and this starts with allowing the Word of God to define Who He is – not your imagination left to itself. When we do this, we see our grandma's god, our denomination's god, or even the religious god of church life. Therefore, during this journey, immerse your mind with the scriptures of who God is. It is also imperative that you relinquish what others have taught you about God. Just set them to the side as you discover the heart of God for yourself. It's not that what you've been told is necessarily false (of which some is), but you want to give God the highest part of your mind so He can impart who He is – TO YOU.

Journey By Faith

In conclusion, though never final, you will find the secret place of the Most High that is reserved for you and God to meet, fellowship, and become one. It is this place of intimacy that satisfies our souls to the fullest. When you discover that secret place, you will want it above life and never miss those appointed times to journey into the heart of God again and again.

Chapter Two

Identifying Your Origin of Faith

Faith that is imputed is about a relationship with God through an unearned position of standard attained through heirship. Abraham is the FATHER of Faith.

My Journey by Faith

Things changed quicker than I could imagine. I had left Selma, AL, headed to Forney, TX. A mutual acquaintance had introduced me to Pastor Marty Reid of Trinity Family Church and had one spot for an RV to hook up. He welcomed me. Little did I realize that COVID would arrive while I was there, extending my stay for 6 months.

If I had to tell you in detail how the Lord provided for me, it wouldn't make sense. He did so with a kingdom algorithm called faith. It supersedes every aspect of the natural realm, and nothing can stop it. Whether a door was opened for me to sell my books or work on a few publishing projects,

Journey By Faith

the Lord took care of me then and continues to do so today. I don't worry. I simply wait, and in my waiting, I rest and enjoy fellowship with the Father. He loves me.

While in Forney, I had access to the church building to get things done. I begin teaching online and even set up a few online courses that taught on spiritual warfare. As I applied my heart and mind to what God was revealing to me, I was becoming more and more acclimated to God's leading. The relationship was deepening. The more intentional we are with God, the more intentional He is with us. You draw near to God; He will draw nearer to you. God loves a challenge, and He loves to be challenged according to His Word. However, we must be sure we are challenging Him back with what He challenged us with – HIS WILL!

It is in the journey that you will discover "YOUR" origin of faith. Like Abraham, it's that 'ah moment' when God appeared to him and told him to leave everything, including his father. When he finally received Isaac, it would happen again only to be asked to sacrifice him on Mt. Moriah. It would take years to learn to totally trust God, and in doing so, Abraham didn't hesitate to offer up Isaac. It was that moment God knew Abraham would trust Him and obey Him fully.

David discovered his origin of faith when he protected the sheep from the lion and the bear. This was why it was only normal for him to confront the uncircumcised Philistine Goliath, behead him, and feed his carcass to the fowls of the air. When God spoke to Moses through a burning bush, changed his staff to a serpent, and his hand to that of a leper, and then back to normal again, it established his origin of faith to confront Pharaoh. (Though he didn't need his brother Aaron to be his spokesperson, God granted him that).

God is no respecter of persons, and He wants to establish you with an anchor, an origin of faith directly related to a mandate that He had ordained for your life before you were even brought forth.

(Jeremiah 1:5) KJV
"Before I formed thee in the belly I knew thee; and before thou camest forth out of the womb I sanctified thee, and I ordained thee a prophet unto the nations."

No other compares to the life of Jesus. Though God in the flesh, He yet embraced by faith HIS journey, which was to die as a forsaken sin offering for the entire world. Everything He did was purposed towards that ONE call. John said it perfectly about Jesus.

(1 John 3:8b) KJV
"<u>For this purpose</u>, the Son of God was manifested, that he might destroy the works of the devil."

The only way Satan's work could be destroyed was to redeem what Adam had lost. The only way that would be possible was there had to be the penalty of death paid for every human being, and ONLY God could qualify for that. He did so by being in Christ, reconciling us to Himself.

Contrary to religious observations, tradition, and decades of teaching on faith for faith, the origin of biblical faith is found in a relationship between God and the individual – YOU! Faith outside of the relationship is nothing but sheer spiritual adultery. It is spiritual deception and rebellion to think one can force God to do something outside His ordained Will which He has purposed in Himself before the foundations of the world.

What exactly is the origin of faith? Why did God establish it to be how every aspect of Himself would be revealed, experienced, and sustained by anyone who would come to Him? Why has faith been the topic of countless teachings, the center of ministries, and yet Jesus Himself declared, when the Son of man returns, will He find faith in the earth?

(Luke 18:8) KJV
[8] "I tell you that he will avenge them speedily. Nevertheless, when the Son of man cometh, shall he find faith on the earth?"

Identifying Your Origin of Faith

Let me be clear; this chapter is solely focused on the origins of faith; NOT what faith is for. Most Christians have been hammered with (Hebrews 11:1) for most of their lives:

(Hebrews 11:1) KJV
[1] "Now faith is the substance of things hoped for, the evidence of things not seen."

Without understanding the origins of faith, the misuse of faith is inevitable. Therefore, it will be applied in a way that is totally out of order of the divine objective – faith FOR what God has willed! It has been diverted towards either the will of man, tradition, or the adversary himself, the devil. There are no other options in this regard. Opinions have no place in the Kingdom of God, and Jesus was emphatic about why He came; to do the Father's Will. He also identified those who are related to Him as those who do God's Will.

(Mark 3:35) KJV
"For whosoever shall do the will of God, the same is my brother, and my sister, and mother."

Therefore, grasping the origins of faith is critical to the primary purpose of faith. When we take an intimate look at the relationship of God and Abraham, there is an unmistakable agenda that God had ordained in coming to Abraham. This is just as true for you and me. Without knowing this, faith has no power in and of itself. Sad to say, many have used faith in a way that is no different than those who use the idea of positive thinking, self-esteem, and other ideologies in which God takes no pleasure. They all are categorized as self-righteousness, which is a filthy rag before a Holy God as ours - Jehovah.

(Isaiah 64:6) KJV
[6] "But we are all as an unclean thing, and all our righteousnesses are as filthy rags; and we all do fade as a leaf; and our iniquities, like the wind, have taken us away."

Furthermore, in our insistence that there is something good in us, we have devised countless schemes to manipulate God into giving us what we want by making it okay for us to do what we want, and that, of course, includes having what we want and when we want it. The heart is simply sick.

(Jeremiah 17:9-10) KJV
[9] "The heart is deceitful above all things, and desperately wicked: who can know it? [10] I the Lord search the heart, I try the reins, even to give every man according to his ways, and according to the fruit of his doings." It is critical to understand the origins of faith. When God established a relationship with Abraham, He did so, requiring Abraham to do ONE thing: Believe Him for what HE said HE would do. In clear language, Abraham believed "what" God said He would do. Abraham had nothing to do with "what" that was. God had decided what that would be.

(Romans 4:3, 20-21) KJV
[3] "For what saith the scripture? Abraham believed God, and it was counted unto him for righteousness. [20] He staggered not at the promise

of God through unbelief; but was strong in faith, giving glory to God; [21] And being fully persuaded that, <u>what he had promised</u>, he was able also to perform."

When we confuse WHO we have faith into the OBJECT that we are having faith, that faith is rendered void. The explicit purpose of biblical faith is to fulfill "what" God has promised. It is not for the "desires of your heart" left uncircumcised and therefore asks to only ask amiss that one may satisfy their own lust.

(James 4:3-4) KJV
[3] "Ye ask, and receive not, because ye ask amiss, that ye may consume it upon your lusts. [4] Ye adulterers and adulteresses, know ye not that the friendship of the world is enmity with God? whosoever therefore will be a friend of the world is the enemy of God."

It is evident as to why the misdirection of faith is being used, friendship with the world. Every aspect of biblical faith is for the Kingdom of God. Jesus is who we are to pattern our life after, Is He not? Listen to what He says:

(Hebrews 10:7, 9) KJV
[7] "Then said I, Lo, I come (in the volume of the book it is written of me,) to do thy will, O God. [9] Then said he, Lo, I come to do thy will, O God. He taketh away the first, that he may establish the second."

(John 5:30) KJV
[30] "I can of mine own self do nothing: as I hear, I judge: and my

judgment is just; because I seek not mine own will, but the will of the Father which hath sent me."

(Matthew 26:42) KJV
[42] "He went away again the second time, and prayed, saying, O my Father, if this cup may not pass away from me, except I drink it, thy will be done."

(Matthew 16:24) KJV
[24] "Then said Jesus unto his disciples, If any man will come after me, let him deny himself, and take up his cross, and follow me."

Countless scriptures establish that faith is solely for the Kingdom of God and the doing of HIS Will. Once a believer fully embraces that they have been chosen to bring forth fruit that directly correlates to God's Will, such faith is then seen as more precious than gold!

(1 Peter 1:7) KJV
[7] "That the trial of your faith, being much more precious than of gold that perisheth, though it be tried with fire, might be found unto praise and honour and glory at the appearing of Jesus Christ:"

What blurs the lines is when we confuse faith with self-determination. Faith is not powered by human flesh! It is a gift from God. He has given every man a proportion of faith and according to the grace related to their particular gift. When we reflect on this prayerfully, what is clear becomes even more explicit:

Faith is the currency of God's Kingdom given to carry out the will of the King.

(Romans 12:6) KJV
[6] "Having then gifts differing according to the grace that is given to us, whether prophecy, let us prophesy according to the proportion of faith;"

(1 Corinthians 12:9a) KJV
"To another faith by the same Spirit;"

Upon closer examination, faith is the deposit of God's confidence and assurance inside of you to carry out what He has given you to do. He knows that what He asks of us is not of the earth, logical, intelligent, common, or in the fashion of and for this world. It is otherworldly and therefore requires the force, confidence, and a "currency" that is literally "given" to us in the same way. Thus, faith is the evidence of the GOD "things" not seen, and GOD "substance" of the GOD "things" hoped for. So let it be clear, it is God through and through.

Does it mean that the desires of our hearts are not essential and relevant to God? Does this suggest that we have nothing to gain in all of this? The answer must be viewed through the timeline of dispensation so we can better understand what it is "time" for, less we find ourselves out of sync with God's timeline.

FAITH DURING THE TIME OF GRACE

God operates within the framework of dispensations. This simply means, His kingdom is all about the kingdom agenda for right now. When we are not in sync with His Kingdom, we ask for things or objectives that it's not time for. Even to the degree that we will never have it in this lifetime. A perfect example of this is those patriarchs of faith found in (Hebrews 11). They accepted that the real promises of God would not be in this life because they were strangers and pilgrims just passing through. They embraced the sufferings, the torture, and even refused deliverance so that they might experience a better resurrection.

What a mindset! Imagine all that we could do in our lives if we just threw off the cares of this life – even if it means death! However, when we have allowed God to establish that origin of faith with us in a personal and intimate way, it happens. It is the only way it will.

(Hebrews 11:13, 35, 39) KJV
"These all died in faith, not having received the promises, but having seen them afar off, and were persuaded of them, and embraced them, and confessed that they were strangers and pilgrims on the earth. [35] Women received their dead raised to life again: and others were tortured, not accepting deliverance; that they might obtain a better resurrection: [39] And these all, having obtained a good report through faith, received not the promise:"

Identifying Your Origin of Faith

"God, I really want this house, and I need the house, that job, that car, that husband, that wife". Is it wrong to ask God for your personal needs? Absolutely not! Heaven hears our request based upon this rule.

(1 John 5:14) KJV
[14] "And this is the confidence that we have in him, that, if we ask any thing according to his will, he heareth us:"

What I am about to say next is probably the single and most straightforward, and essential principle in the realm of faith because it aligns all scripture with being placed in the proper framework to be applied in our own personal journey in life:

Faith operates within the mysterious and intimate place of a personal relationship of obedience with God the Father through His Son, Jesus Christ that desires to fulfill His will on the earth.

I want to emphasize "with God". I can fill this section with countless scripture to establish so many of these truths; however, without setting the cornerstone of the relationship rooted in obedience, scripture has no relevance whatsoever. So many have wrestled the scriptures to their own destruction attempting to manipulate the Kingdom of God to fit their own individual agenda or desires – by faith.

(2 Peter 3:16) KJV
[16] "As also in all his epistles, speaking in them of these things; in which are some things hard to be understood, which they that are unlearned and unstable wrest, as they do also the other scriptures, unto their own destruction."

Likewise, many insist on a relationship with the scriptures, but not with Jesus, Who is the Word made flesh.

(John 5:40) KJV
[39] "Search the scriptures; for in them ye think ye have eternal life: and they are they which testify of me. [40] And ye will not come to me, that ye might have life."

The axiom on which we must stand when addressing God in prayer is:

(Matthew 26:42) KJV
[42] "He went away again the second time, and prayed, saying, <u>O my Father, if this cup may not pass away from me, except I drink it, thy will be done.</u>"

Are you bearing the cup that God has given you? The cup represents the burden that God has commissioned you to carry in this life. Knowing what that cup is – is not enough. Doing it is all that matters because faith without works is dead.

(James 2:17-18) KJV
[17] "Even so faith, if it hath not works, is dead, being alone. [18] Yea, a man may say, Thou hast faith, and I have works: shew me thy faith without thy works, and I will shew thee my faith by my works."

Identifying Your Origin of Faith

The culture of Christianity in our generation is all about learning, knowing, discussing, debating, or arguing a doctrinal position. However, when you do a sum of all the effort given to these preparatory measures, very little time is spent doing His revealed Will measurably and tangibly. And doing it NOW! It's like being in a boot camp for training, but you never leave boot camp to get in the actual game. At best, we transfer to another boot camp for more training or more knowledge. The boot camps are all over the place and even online.

- Bible College
- Seminary
- Faith Workshops
- Another church Bible class on faith
- Joining a new church

Hebrews puts this in clear language when it declares that there is a time when we ought to be teachers and that only through use can the senses be exercised to discern good and evil.

(Hebrews 5:12-14) KJV
[12] "For when for the time ye ought to be teachers, ye have need that one teach you again which be the first principles of the oracles of God; and are become such as have need of milk, and not of strong meat. [13] For every one that useth milk is unskilful in the word of righteousness: for he

is a babe. [14] But strong meat belongeth to them that are of full age, even those who by <u>reason of use</u> have their senses exercised to discern both good and evil."

It should be clear that no amount of learning will replace doing. In fact, it is the actual doing that teaches because faith is an impartation from a living God, not a stagnant idea taught by men. Therefore, God always took His people on a journey. If it wasn't to possess the land, it was a wilderness experience for disobedience. If not the wilderness, it was to stir up complacency. No matter the calling, God's classroom is a call to "exercise" so that you may learn to discern both good and evil. Any mechanic will tell you a car unused will eventually be of no use. Even so, faith not used will die.

Discovering your origin of faith must be pursued with a hunger and a thirst that supersedes anyone and everything else in life. It is the field that you sell everything to buy. It is what you engage in spiritual warfare against wicked spirits to obtain and to protect.

Satan does not want you to discover your origin of faith. He will do all he can do to keep you from discovering your origin of faith. He will offer you religion, cars, status, friends, pleasure, and the best that the kingdom of this world has to offer because he recognizes, more than we do, the eternal value and the potent power of a faith that is rooted in

YOUR origin, YOUR purpose, and YOUR spiritual DNA. Remember, he lived in the very presence of God, and he operated in his purpose, and therefore he tasted this realm of life. We can't even imagine the glory and the majesty that Lucifer experienced. What he had been given access to by faith supersedes to untold levels what he knew before being cast out of heaven. We will share new heaven and a new earth. Therefore, he will use the entire arsenal of whiles and schemes to hinder you during his limited time on earth.

How to identify your origin of faith

(Romans 12:1-2) KJV
[1] "I beseech you therefore, brethren, by the mercies of God, that ye present your bodies a living sacrifice, holy, acceptable unto God, which is your reasonable service. [2] And be not conformed to this world: but be ye transformed by the renewing of your mind, that ye may prove what is that good, and acceptable, and perfect, will of God."

Your Body

Your body will be directly attached to you being able to ascertain the will of God. I cannot make it more straightforward than that. There is an attack against living for God that is coming from many false teachers and preachers. I don't get it! With all the emphasis on the grace of God to NOT lose your salvation (of which I believe is a lie from the most bottomless pit of hell), why isn't it more zealous and joyous in teaching why you don't have to sin because of grace and that through Christ we're dead to it?! Besides, if you love someone, why have a mind to try to get away with hurting them and still think you can be in a meaningful relationship. It just doesn't add up.

Anyway, this is not the place to take on this doctrine that totally does despite the spirit of grace and tramples underfoot the blood of this most precious covenant and puts to open shame the crucifixion of Christ. It is impossible to renew to repentance one who has done so. What couldn't be clearer that a living soul can go the way of Lucifer and the fallen angels than faithfully embracing the way of Christ? I digress with the following scripture.

(Hebrews 6:4-6) KJV
[4] "For it is impossible for those who were once enlightened, and have tasted of the heavenly gift, and were made partakers of the Holy Ghost, [5] And have tasted the good word of God, and the powers of the world to come, [6] If they shall fall away, to renew them again unto repentance; seeing they crucify to themselves the Son of God afresh and put him to an open shame."

Back to your body...

If you want to know what the perfect Will of God is, it starts with a sacrifice that is willing and a pursuit of the Kingdom of God that is deliberate. As you are then transformed by renewing your mind, there will begin an unveiling and a revealing of God's perfect Will. It is intimate, personal, and unmistakable. Be sure of this: It will cost you everything that hinders you from obtaining, and everyone who would distract you from fulfilling His Will. This is how Paul considered what it cost him:

(Philippians 3:8) KJV
[8] "Yea doubtless, and I count all things but loss for the excellency of the knowledge of Christ Jesus my Lord: for whom I have suffered the loss of all things, and do count them but dung, that I may win Christ,"

- This is about winning Christ.
- This is about preparing for eternity.
- This is about attaining to the righteousness of God BY faith
- This is about abandoning my and others' self-righteousness by works religion and guilt.
- This is about embracing the sufferings that have been delegated to me by His sovereign Will.
- This is about living a true biblical life rooted in a biblical faith that transcends any and everything this life has to offer.

This list of "about" can fill this and other books without end because it lifts us up from this temporal realm into eternity. It has even given me the sense of urgency to write this book.

Journey By Faith

Your Origin of Faith in Summary

So, are you ready to draw near to God so that He would draw nearer to you? Are you prepared to count the cost and set your affections on things above that you may be able to comprehend what He comprehends of you? Are you putting your sites on the new heaven and the new earth, of which the birth pains reveal is soon?

There are no shortcuts, and there doesn't need to be. Through Christ, we can attain right now what He has made available to us through FAITH. A faith that works by love, not the law of works. So many of God's people have made complicated what is so simple. The simplicity of it can only come through the faith of a child.

(Matthew 18:2-3) KJV
"And Jesus called a little child unto him, and set him in the midst of them, [3] And said, Verily I say unto you, Except ye be converted, and become as little children, ye shall not enter into the kingdom of heaven."

No one can know what God has for you – But God. Let me reiterate.

NO ONE CAN KNOW WHAT GOD HAS FOR YOU – BUT GOD!

(Hebrews 8:11) KJV
"And they shall not teach every man his neighbour, and every man his brother, saying, Know the Lord: for all shall know me, from the least to the greatest,"

This means you must come to Him to get it. It doesn't matter how many prophecies you are told, how often you attend church, what your pastor tells you, or how much you are assured of your salvation and even doctrine that you have come to learn. You still must RISE UP and go get the Will of God for your life. Once you obtain it by faith, you must start living it by faith. You must press into the kingdom of God with everything that is in you. The kingdom of heaven suffers violence, and only the spiritual violent will and can take it by force. If there is no spiritual fervor in your life - you have no fire. If there is no suffering and enduring, then you are living in a passive state of spirituality. You are perhaps tethering on lukewarmness and find yourself of little to no zeal for the things of God. You must return to your first love!

The Drudgery of Church Life

Today's church generation uses church like a baby uses a pacifier. They are being satisfied by merely the act of getting the substance, but there is nothing there. Let's be honest, most churches today are maintaining or just living in a state of repeat. Build another church and plant another one to just put one of "their sons" there to teach the same thing. The most challenging part in the local church today to accept is that many well-meaning pastors have simply been inoculated to the religious vaccine of complacency. They have settled to keep the people sedated by refusing to confront sin, stir conviction, and create a heart for the lost, and above all to discover God's WILL for their own lives and pursue it.

The great commission has been replaced with the tremendous counterfeit gospel. Jesus is presented as a mere person of soft soulish lovely dovely, anything goes affection and not a fierce KING who demands loyalty according to His grace that works in us by love. We hear the part of the gospel that tells us, "God so loved the world that He gave His only begotten son." Yet we never hear, "Depart from me ye that work iniquity, I never knew you!" Perhaps I haven't addressed this portion with perfect balance, or you're just immature to accept these truths; whatever the case, the falling away from the faith is in full swing. I can only pray that you are working out your own salvation with fear and trembling and are prepared to answer for your life before a holy and righteous God. When each of us does, there will be no one standing there – not even your pastor.

I encourage you to rekindle the fire. Go back to your first love. Discover your origin of faith and then pursue God, and He will pursue you. Run from churches that are sedating you with soft words and fair speech, but their heart is for themselves, and they need your substance which includes your money and your passions to sustain it.

(Matthew 11:12) KJV
"And from the days of John the Baptist until now the kingdom of heaven suffereth violence, and the violent take it by force."

Chapter Three

Your Journey Starts With a Step of Faith

It was March 24, 2019, the morning of my second bike tour that would cover 3,000 miles from coast to coast, sharing the gospel with whoever came in my path. I am anticipating God's presence that only manifested in such ways when I launched out into the deep of doing His Will. I had experienced Him on my first bike tour, and I wanted it again. I needed it. I came to realize that doing God's will is true "meat," as Jesus said.

(John 4:34) KJV
"Jesus saith unto them, My meat is to do the will of him that sent me, and to finish his work."

It was meat because it satisfied my essence. It was the very thing I was born to do, and I knew it. It went beyond mere "discussing" the things of God. It was not another theological exegesis (of which I've never done anyway). It was beyond food for the stomach; it was the abundant life that Jesus spoke of and would only be possible to experience by doing His will. His will is a journey.

After attending a conference in Anaheim, CA, that same month, I would start the second adventure of riding my bike from coast to coast. My first tour was over 1,000 miles from Nevada to Texas. Unfortunately, I couldn't finish it due to back fatigue, and my bike tour ended in Sweetwater, TX. I was enthused with this new bike tour and could not wait for my first encounter with Jesus and with a soul who needed to hear of Him.

Little did I realize on the morning of my launch; it would not be. I heard the Lord whisper, "No, William." I blocked it out because I was already in California, and my mind was set. I had shipped my bike, attended a conference, promoted my launch, had a book signing for my new book, "Astonished", that told of my first bike tour, and it was time to go! Not only was I having issues with my Alexis Heel, but God's voice was a bit louder than a whisper now. It was like, I could see Him plucking some grape-like heavenly snack with one hand and His other on my forehead saying, "Not so, my son." Of course, He had one of those smiles you can't really comprehend. It would be of joy that I wanted to go for Him, but His eyebrows would reflect, "Chill out, boy, I got a better plan, you know." I left Him eating His grapes and headed to the beach to start my bike tour. Lovingly defiant.

Your Journey Starts with a Step of Faith

So, at the beach with a few friends gathered around me for prayer and a few songs, my mind was trying to process how I would climb these hills with the condition I was dealing with. I reasoned short daily trips would suffice. I didn't care if it took me a few years to do this bike trek; I wanted to experience God again the way I did on my last journey. I needed to Astonish Him again. It was time to start my ride, and as I rounded the public restroom (out of sight from those who were there), my front tire shifted in the sand; bam - I was on the ground! No one saw me but three old men sitting together on a bench. One of them said, "It looks like you're off to not that good of a start." (Now that I think of it, they look like angles who were probably 800 years old each). God said, "William, I see your heart, my son, consider your desire to make this bike journey as done before me. I have ordained another journey for you at this time in your life." I sighed, but inside, I cried.

At that instant, the morning experience came rushing back to my mind. It was like my eye dilated to 10, and the rewind happened until I arrived back in the driveway just 1 hour ago. How could I miss it!

As I packed the SUV of a brother in the Lord who came out to transport me to the beach, the next-door neighbor and I had a brief and pleasant encounter. We exchanged hellos, and she expressed that she had heard about what I was doing and thought it was terrific. I gave God the praise. In a passing statement, I said to her, "That's a nice rig you have on the side of your house." She immediately said, "Oh that!" I am tired of it and want it off my Property." She added, "I'll sell it to you for a really good price!"

As I expressed to her my journey on the bike and being in full-time ministry, in passing and without thought, I asked if she'd take a taxi write-off. She immediately said, "Yes!" I was floored. Even then, after God told me with a whisper, "No" that morning, I still couldn't see clearly yet what God was doing. He was rewarding my faith before I could even get to the beach and start my tour. He provided for me because He knew I was not going on this bike for over a year and 3,000 miles.

Back to the beach....

I lifted myself up off the ground quickly before my guest could see what had happened. I climbed back on my bike and kept riding as if I was going. As they shot the video, my mind raced at what was unfolding all within the last few hours. God first whispered, "No." Then having SAID, "No," God had given me a motorhome, and He had gently laid me down on the ground and said, "William, I have another journey for you at this time in your life. No, my child.

Okay. I got the message.

I needed a place to stay for the night. The home where I was hosted had just received new missionaries for a week or so. I had to rest my mind and reset. Somehow break the news to everyone and craft a story that made sense. So naturally, my Achilles Heel would be a more logical narrative. So be it. It was true, and more so than I thought, I wouldn't have made it 20 miles. I started treatment with a chiropractor the next day. To find a place, I logged on to www.warmshowers.org to see what I could find. It's a community that lets you find other cyclists who will let you crash in their homes for a few days. It usually takes a week or so to find someone that can accommodate you. Well, I found that person in few minutes. He gave me his address, and I started peddling to his home, which was not that far away. When I looked at the address, it made my eyebrows rise. Anyway, I was on my way.

I couldn't believe it!

I was back on the street that I had just left. I counted the houses, and the motorhome that the neighbor had just given me was 7 houses away from where I was standing, and

Journey By Faith

I could see the RV! The name of the street was Nevada. Oh yeah, Nevada was the first state that I started my first tour from! This was a miracle. Here I was in Huntington Beach, CA, with millions of residences and the very street I just left, I was back on. God simply looked at me with that loving look as He popped another grape like delight in His mouth.

My host took me to dinner, then he took me to get a much-needed massage. The next day, he gave me a brand-new iPhone for my new journey! God was comforting me – it worked.

Within a month, I was in the RV. Suffice to say, getting the RV was one miracle. There were numerous others for it to transition from the side of the house to me driving it. The owner spent $2,000 of her own money to have it towed to the Ford dealership. They had to find out why it wouldn't start and fix it. Once they received it, I sat down with the owners. I told them I was a missionary to America and didn't expect this to be given an RV. Before they spend time on it, they needed to be aware of my circumstances. They understood and proceeded with servicing it. Within a week, I contacted them and told them it was the only transportation I had. They told me to come up and gave me a brand-new truck to use! Cool God. It even synced with my phone. I used it to sleep in most of the time as well.

Finally, about three weeks later, they had it fixed. I showed up to be given an invoice for $4,000! I went straight to the owners and reminded them of our conversation. They took it down to $1,500 and told me to pay what I could today and pay it out over time. I gave them $200, and that's what I did.

It would take two weeks after being in this incredible, practically new 36 ft. RV with only 49,000 miles for me to realize what God had done for me. On that day, when I woke up in a very comfortable bed, I cried. After seeing so many homeless people sleeping in their cars and tents, I realized just how faithful God had been to me and how He honored my faith in Him.

This would be experienced that I became fully persuaded to believe that there is no other way to live than by faith. So, it is good, divine, and an honor for the Just to live by FAITH!

I pray my testimony encourages you to be assured that God has you covered.

Journey By Faith

It's not an option because we don't need one

Living by faith in Who God is, what He has done, and what He has promised to do according to His Will is not an option. Let me emphasize the word SHALL. Nonetheless, we go about attempting to arrange our lives in a way that will have no risk, no out of "our control" circumstances, and absolutely no suffering. This is called "religion" that has a form of godliness. Still, it denies the power of God by avoiding trusting God, Who loves us and gave Himself for us through His Son, Jesus Christ.

Imagine that! Going through all the motions of religion: church attendance, tithe, and offering (out of obligation), studying theology, getting degrees, pastoring churches, taking communion, and more don't guarantee our trust in God. There are even couples who get married for the express purpose of ministry and not because they genuinely love each other. The list goes on and on and on. Yet, there is no intimate relationship validated by a witness of trust that can only be demonstrated by your faith in Him that reaches beyond mere confession. A faith that is evident by those works that He has given you to do. He will perform it through you according to what He has purposed you for before the foundations of the world.

(Hebrews 11:6) KJV
"But without faith it is impossible to please him: for he that cometh to

God must believe that he is, and that he is a rewarder of them that diligently seek him."

It is a problem when the scriptures are interpreted outside of knowing the agape love of God. When not knowing this love, we hear this scripture as a voice of duty and command. It is hard for us to imagine it coming from a loving Father saying, "Hey, and by the way, don't worry about all the issues of life. I'll provide all of that for you. I love you so much; you shall simply live by faith. I'm going to meet your needs according to my riches in glory that is in Christ Jesus! So, flow with me and take no thought for your life, seek first my kingdom, and just live by faith as you pursue my will for your life because it's part of the deal. I got you. I really do."

When we read this command coming from love – it is a freedom to live by faith! Human nature has constantly challenged God and believes it knows how to do what God has revealed His Will to be. There are many Bible stories of those who went about doing God's Will their way only to experience catastrophic results and even heartbreak. I think of Sampson. In fact, I watched the newest version of the movie last night. It was a good movie and revealed just how stubborn we can be. I saw parts of my heart in there as well.

Nonetheless, we insist on methods that reflect a core issue with trusting God in every area of our lives. This is especially true with those intimate areas of work, marriage, houses, cars, and the cares of this life, especially money.

(Romans 1:17) KJV
[17] "For therein is the righteousness of God revealed from faith to faith: as it is written, The just shall live by faith."

When I imagine heaven, I do so with one theme in mind. It will fully display my faith in God by the reward I receive from Him because the fire will try every man's work.

(1 Corinthians 3:15) KJV
"If any man's work shall be burned, he shall suffer loss: but he himself shall be saved; yet so as by fire."

Fire does not discriminate. It simply burns what can be burned. When faith has been released and produced fruit in your life, it will withstand the fire. As well, when you have not pursued what God has invited you to pursue, fire will reveal that also. It will be the wood, hay, and stubble which will burn quickly.

Nothing can be simpler than to accept that the just has been set free to live by faith. Faith is the evidence of things not seen; it is the substance of things hoped for (Hebrews 11:1). It is the evidence of your food, shelter, resources, vision, strength, the people God has for you, and every provision you will need throughout your life. It is provided for when your heart is set on doing the will of God. Whether physical, psychological, emotional, or spiritual, faith is the currency of heaven. All you need to start is the faith that is the size of a mustard seed. It can move a mountain when you know you are in the Will of God. Without the Will of God, faith is merely an idea that will make God do nothing.

How to Initiate Your Faith

Initiate your faith NOW by taking that step towards the vision God has placed in your spirit. Whatever it is, just begin to do it. It could be writing the first sentence of the book God has revealed to you. Perhaps it is as simple as obeying His direction of turning off the TV and coming off social media to spend time with Him in prayer. Faith is not always doing. Many times, it is not doing the things that take away from you. You must discover your own rhythm of faith that is rooted in a relationship. This is only possible by spending deliberate and intimate time with God in both His Word and His presence.

It will be out of this secret place that your faith will begin to rise, and as you obey in faith, revelation will come your way. It is not a revelation of end times, what is happening in the world, or even in the church. It is a Rhema word for you. Rhema means "an utterance." It is a particular and intimate

Journey By Faith

knowledge that God wants you to have as it pertains to your life at this very moment. The Psalmist calls it the secret place of the Most High. It's called the secret place for a reason. So, often, we are quick to run and tell everything we know about God or what He has revealed to us. It is not possible for them to understand, nor is it for them. The faith we obtain is in direct collation to the relationship we develop with our Heavenly Father, Jesus as our Savior, and the Word of God. It is impossible to sit in His presence, reflect on His Word, and not have your faith increased.

(Romans 10:17) KJV
"So then faith cometh by hearing, and hearing by the word of God."

Don't complicate the simplicity that is in Christ Jesus. Therefore this life of faith has to be approached with the attitude of a child. Suppose you try to intellectualize this process or take a religious approach. In that case, you will fail because God will have no flesh to glory in His presence.

(1 Corinthians 1:26-29) KJV
"For ye see your calling, brethren, how that not many wise men after the flesh, not many mighty, not many noble, are called: [27] But God hath chosen the foolish things of the world to confound the wise; and God hath chosen the weak things of the world to confound the things which are mighty; [28] And base things of the world, and things which are despised, hath God chosen, yea, and things which are not, to bring to nought things that are: [29] That no flesh should glory in his presence."

What will be the first step you take? Rest assured; He has already gone before you. Go!

Your Own Righteousness

It stinks, repulsive before God, and is rude to oneself and others. It is the cause of conflict in every sector of life, whether domestically, socially, or politically. You can add any other sector of society not mentioned. Self-righteousness has especially manifested itself within our culture that has taken it to a new low. This has deepened the racial divide, sexual redefining by preference, and even the rule of law being flipped on one's head.

Self-righteousness places us way above where we should be placing ourselves, or it buries us beneath the ground as dead and totally unworthy to receive anything from God. So how do we obtain a balanced view of who we are and the value of this?

Let's get a proper definition of self-righteousness first. In the most straightforward way, I can put it, self-righteousness is placing trust in yourself. Whether subtle, arrogantly, or through false humility, you will control the narrative by setting the rules about yourself and others. To even begin to move in this direction, the person must somehow believe there is something inherently good in themselves. From there, they then establish some form of "good deed" that highlights that it's good.

Point and case. There was a little boy who was a mischievous lad. His dad loved him immensely. He reminded him of himself in so many ways, and yet there was one issue the little boy struggled with, and that was doing his choirs of taking out the garbage. He always had a rationale for justifying why it wasn't done this week. To anchor down his argument, he would always do something extra to compensate for his disobedience. His self-righteousness was working very effectively, though, he thought. It would take time, but his loving father would not compromise with him and corrected him with the appropriate consequences. It finally sank in one day when the son asked the father, "Why don't you like the things that I do for you even when I do wrong?" The father replied, "Son, I don't like you because of what you do or don't do. When you obey my voice, that's the only way I know you like me too."

You see, we think that God loves us because of what we choose to do and not what He asks of us. So, we want to set the rules when we try to depend on our self-regulated ways. In essence, we are telling God, I don't like your ways, and I just think my way is better.

There is no quicker way to nullify faith than through self-righteous acts. Thus, at the root of self is the motive of not trusting God's Word, and therefore, being ignorant of the righteousness of God, we go about establishing our own.

(Romans 10:3) KJV
[3] "For they being ignorant of God's righteousness, and going about to establish their own righteousness, have not submitted themselves unto the righteousness of God."

When we submit ourselves to the righteousness of God, we can rest, and literally, cease from our own self-righteousness and receive the redemptive work done by Christ upon the cross. However, it is easier said than done because every religion and denomination has created some form of added "necessity" to complete and compete with what Jesus has done. Whether it is going to their Bible College, spending 2 years on a mission trip, serving the bishop, or never missing a Sunday or Wednesday night Bible study; one might be responsible for such addition. While some of these expressions are a part of the Christian heritage, they become void when we use them to replace a relationship. They are man's creation to justify ourselves before God in some form or fashion. Ultimately, it is the devil working deceit upon hearts not fully submitted to God.

Obedience that works by Faith

(1 Samuel 15:22) KJV
"And Samuel said, Hath the LORD as great delight in burnt offerings and sacrifices, as in obeying the voice of the LORD? Behold, to obey is better than sacrifice, and to hearken than the fat of rams."

What is the motive behind self-righteousness? The most straightforward answer I can give: to justify disobedience. You can slice it and dice it a thousand ways. The bottom line is to find a way to avoid obeying God. His written commandments and that specific will that He has revealed to your heart and mind in some measure. God is aiming to get us to a place of steadfast obedience. This requires a faith that is not stagnant nor religious. <u>The just shall live by faith</u> starts over every day and then throughout the day because you are actively choosing to be obedient to God's leading right NOW!

While in Pensacola, FL (which is this very moment as I write the book) I developed a schedule that included sharing poetry and playing my djembe on the street downtown. It was a great way to share the gospel, and people also blessed me with contributions. This day, God spoke to me and said today, "I want you to work on the book and the video lesson, not to minister with your Djembe and poetry." The sun was out, and I knew it would have been a great day to set up, so I persuaded myself that I can spend a few hours doing so and then write. Then the Lord said, "Don't peddle your gift; I will provide for you. Work on your book and video today." I said, "Yes, Lord," and got to work. In other words, I obeyed. My djembe and poetry had to take their proper place. It is easy to make your gift or talent that God has given you, what you do, and not the specific will that God has called you to fulfill. Gifts and talents are tools that God will use but don't confuse them with the specific will that God wants them to be used for. Pots and pans are gifts, but the meal is the will.

Therefore, more time is needed in His Word and in His presence. It doesn't matter if you're doing poetry on the street or building a skyscraper; God wants obedience to HIS WILL. In the secret place of the MOST HIGH, your origin of faith is established, and God's voice is heard. Hearing God's voice is not audible; (though some have been blessed to hear His audible voice) it is spiritual. It is developed over time, and when you establish this rhythm of life and relationship, you will want no other life than that of living by faith in obeying God's voice.

King Saul had persuaded himself that keeping the best of the animals was relevant to his own agenda. And the establishing of a political relationship with King Agag was somehow important. Notice that he kept everything that was good and destroyed all that was vile. That should give you an indication that his motive was based on carnal benefits.

(1 Samuel 15:9) KJV '
'But Saul and the people spared Agag, and the best of the sheep, and of the oxen, and of the fatlings, and the lambs, and all that was good, and would not utterly destroy them: but everything that was vile and refuse, that they destroyed utterly."

Where do you and I fit in this story? Perhaps you have read this passage many times, but please let it read you.

(1 Samuel 15:13-35) KJV
"And Samuel came to Saul: and Saul said unto him, Blessed be thou of the LORD: I have performed the commandment of the LORD. [14] And Samuel said, What meaneth then this bleating of the sheep in mine ears, and the lowing of the oxen which I hear? [15] And Saul said, They have brought them from the Amalekites: for the people spared the best of the sheep and of the oxen, to sacrifice unto the LORD thy God; and the rest we have utterly destroyed. [16] Then Samuel said unto Saul, Stay, and I will tell thee what the LORD hath said to me this night. And he said unto him, Say on. [17] And Samuel said, When thou wast little in thine own sight, wast thou not made the head of the tribes of Israel, and the LORD anointed thee king over Israel? [18] And the LORD sent thee on a journey, and said, Go and utterly destroy the sinners the Amalekites, and fight against them until they be consumed. [19] Wherefore then didst thou not obey the voice of the LORD, but didst fly upon the spoil, and didst evil in the sight of the LORD? [20] And Saul said unto Samuel, Yea, I have obeyed the voice of the LORD, and have gone the way which the LORD sent me, and have brought Agag the king of Amalek, and have utterly destroyed the Amalekites. [21] But the people took of the spoil, sheep and oxen, the chief of the things which should have been utterly destroyed, to sacrifice unto the LORD thy God in Gilgal. [22] And Samuel

said, Hath the LORD as great delight in burnt offerings and sacrifices, as in obeying the voice of the LORD? Behold, to obey is better than sacrifice, and to hearken than the fat of rams. [23] For rebellion is as the sin of witchcraft, and stubbornness is as iniquity and idolatry. Because thou hast rejected the word of the LORD, he hath also rejected thee from being king. [24] And Saul said unto Samuel, I have sinned: for I have transgressed the commandment of the LORD, and thy words: because I feared the people, and obeyed their voice. [25] Now therefore, I pray thee, pardon my sin, and turn again with me, that I may worship the LORD. [26] And Samuel said unto Saul, I will not return with thee: for thou hast rejected the word of the LORD, and the LORD hath rejected thee from being king over Israel. [27] And as Samuel turned about to go away, he laid hold upon the skirt of his mantle, and it rent. [28] And Samuel said unto him, The LORD hath rent the kingdom of Israel from thee this day, and hath given it to a neighbour of thine, that is better than thou. [29] And also the Strength of Israel will not lie nor repent: for he is not a man, that he should repent. [30] Then he said, I have sinned: yet honour me now, I pray thee, before the elders of my people, and before Israel, and turn again with me, that I may worship the LORD thy God. [31] So Samuel turned again after Saul; and Saul worshipped the LORD. [32] Then said Samuel, Bring ye hither to me Agag the king of the Amalekites. And Agag came unto him delicately. And Agag said, Surely the bitterness of death is past. [33] And Samuel said, As thy sword hath made women childless, so shall thy mother be childless among women. And Samuel hewed Agag in pieces before the LORD in Gilgal. [34] Then Samuel went to Ramah; and Saul went up to his house to Gibeah of Saul. [35] And Samuel came no more to see Saul until the day of his death: nevertheless Samuel mourned for Saul: and the LORD repented that he had made Saul king over Israel."

I could go into detail on this section; however, I simply want to highlight serval key points.

I have performed the commandment of the LORD.

Disobedience is always rooted in self-righteous behavior, which justifies itself with religious works. Saul had premeditated his actions and reasons and somehow came up with a different outcome than God had told him. He arrogantly said, "I have performed the commandment of the Lord," and that after he greeted Samuel with, "Praise the Lord, brother prophet, glory to God! Hallelujah! He had persuaded himself that his sacrifice would nullify the instructions of God. Many churches have been built, songs sang, missionary trips made, and even people getting married only to justify disobeying God. It is a vain attempt to rewrite the specific instructions that God has given us either through His Word and directly.

And also the Strength of Israel will not lie nor repent: for he is not a man that he should repent.

God will not change His mind on what He has called you to do and how He has called you to do it. He is perfect. He is glorious. His is All-Powerful, All-Knowing, Omnipotent, Omnipresent, and Love itself. So why would He need to change His mind? His ways are perfect. Therefore, for us to seek to do it our way, it reveals the human heart's very repulsiveness. We, therefore, being ignorant of the righteousness of God, seek to establish our own even as Saul did. He insisted that he did obey God until he realized that the Word of the Lord could not, nor would it, be altered through the prophet Samuel.

People will push you to agree with their disobedience and rebellious ways, and when you don't, they will cut you off with a quickness! Instead, each of us should have a clear word from the Lord as to His purpose for our lives. In doing so, we enter into our own journey by faith.

The danger of tempting God in the Old Testament was evident in many ways. He was known for outright killing thousands of people for sin. Let us not think that there are consequences for doing so today.

(1 Corinthians 10:9) KJV
[9] "Neither let us tempt Christ, as some of them also tempted, and were destroyed of serpents.

1 Corinthians 10:9 AMP
[9] We must not tempt the Lord [that is, test His patience, question His purpose or exploit His goodness], as some of them did and they were killed by serpents."

We make a grave mistake when we tempt Christ thinking that the New Testament expression of grace can be trifled with! So many have thought they could usurp the authority of Jesus and even do despite to the spirit of grace and trample it underfoot without consequence.

(Hebrews 2:2-3) KJV
"For if the word spoken by angels was steadfast, and every transgression and disobedience received a just recompense of reward; [3] How shall we escape, if we neglect so great salvation; which at the first began to be spoken by the Lord, and was confirmed unto us by them that heard him;"

(Hebrews 10:28-31) KJV
"He that despised Moses' law died without mercy under two or three witnesses: [29] Of how much sorer punishment, suppose ye, shall he be thought worthy, who hath trodden under foot the Son of God, and hath counted the blood of the covenant, wherewith he was sanctified, an unholy thing, and hath done despite unto the Spirit of grace? [30] For we know him that hath said, Vengeance belongeth unto me, I will recompense, saith the Lord. And again, The Lord shall judge his people. [31] It is a fearful thing to fall into the hands of the living God."

How much clearer can the scripture be? There is a direct correlation between the Old Testament judgment and New Testament grace. A severer judgment is to be administered to those who trodden underfoot the Son of God! Yet when He has given one over to a reprobate mind, they can no longer discern good from evil and only wrestle the scriptures to their own destruction.

(2 Peter 3:16) KJV
"As also in all his epistles, speaking in them of these things; in which are some things hard to be understood, which they that are unlearned and unstable wrest, as they do also the other scriptures, unto their own destruction."

Your Journey Starts with a Step of Faith

The most heart-wrenching reality is that one can be rejected by God when one insists on rebelling against Him. It is on equal standing with witchcraft because we seek to evoke control over our own lives through spiritual means outside of spirit and truth, which only comes by Jesus Christ.

1 Samuel 15:23 KJV
For rebellion is as the sin of witchcraft, and stubbornness is as iniquity and idolatry. Because thou hast rejected the word of the LORD, he hath also rejected thee from being king.

I will guarantee you that this path will always show up when we deviate from spending time in God's Word and on our face in humility. While there are millions upon millions of resources of biblical knowledge available today, if there is no contrite heart and broken spirit before Him, it accounts for nothing. Never have we had so much "revelation of the scriptures" and so little exploits of faith in our generation. Why is it like that? Because our own self-righteousness has found means to keep Agag alive and to enjoy the best of the land while claiming, "I have obeyed God."

Who is your King Agag?

Maybe your Agag has been your career, your education, your status, or your business. Whatever it is, God told you that wasn't what He told you to do, but you found reason to keep it alive so that you could benefit from it. You didn't want to trust

God. Unfortunately, we fall prey to putting our trust in this temporal life. We store up treasures that will eventually be corrupted and have little or absolutely no affinity for the eternal reign to come. Rather, we have not stored up for ourselves treasures for the life to come, which will never end. Believe me, I've heard it all, and it all sounds good and reasonable in its justifications. However, what will it matter on that horrible Day of Judgment when we do make it into heaven? What will you have to show for your faith while on the earth, or will you make it by fire?

(1 Corinthians 3:15) KJV
"If any man's work shall be burned, he shall suffer loss: but he himself shall be saved; yet so as by fire."

If you intend to embrace the discovery of God's will, you must have the right mindset to do so. It cannot include having love for the things of this world because it will never permit you to embrace God's Will.

(1 John 2:15-17) KJV
"Love not the world, neither the things that are in the world. If any man love the world, the love of the Father is not in him. [16] For all that is in the world, the lust of the flesh, and the lust of the eyes, and the pride of life, is not of the Father, but is of the world. [17] And the world passeth away, and the lust thereof: but he that doeth the will of God abideth for ever."

Affections are lethal! Yet when you set them on things above by rendering your life dead, you then come into a revelation that true life is being hidden in Christ, and that is life everlasting! That enables you to live without apology or explain yourself to people because your works will speak for you.

(Colossians 3:1-3) KJV
"If ye then be risen with Christ, seek those things which are above, where Christ sitteth on the right hand of God. [2] Set your affection on things above, not on things on the earth. [3] For ye are dead, and your life is hid with Christ in God."

What is your bleating sheep?

Are they houses, cars, or materialism? Consumed with just keeping what you have afloat while trying to get a few more things every month, even if it means getting a part-time job to pay for it. You might think, I'm suggesting that you don't have a house and just walk to places. Well, I'm not. The point I'm making is that when there is no contentment with what you have, and yet you want more of what you in essence already have, you have succumbed to the bleating of the sheep!

Unfortunately, most Christians in America just don't have the time to truly seek God and obey Him because they have weighed themselves down with stuff. They have too much, owe too much, and worry too much. There is no time to simply seek first the Kingdom of God and HIS righteousness.

Therefore, by default, we work to possess things just like the world, and go to church on Sunday to soothe our spiritually boring lives.

There is so much more in this story of King Saul because it parallels our own propensities as human beings. I, therefore, admonish you to take a moment to meditate on this story and ask the Holy Spirit to show you – you.

Keep one element to this entire journey in the center of your spirit and mind: God is not going to make you do anything for Him. He wants a WILLING and OBEDIENT heart. That means only through sacrificial living can you take this journey by faith. Only through a surrendered life can you live by faith. If you intend to discover God's Will and do it, then be prepared to suffer, be rejected, be alone (but not), be misunderstood, and be without while yet possessing everything you need. God wants to separate you from every hindrance in your life to transition you into His liberty and freedom.

(1 Corinthians 6:12) KJV
"All things are lawful unto me, but all things are not expedient: all things are lawful for me, but I will not be brought under the power of any."

(Philippians 3:8-15) KJV
"Yea doubtless, and I count all things but loss for the excellency of the knowledge of Christ Jesus my Lord: for whom I have suffered the loss of all things, and do count them but dung, that I may win Christ, [9] And be found in him, not having mine own righteousness, which is of the law, but that which is through the faith of Christ, the righteousness which is of God by faith: [10] That I may know him, and the power of his resurrection, and the fellowship of his sufferings, being made conformable unto

his death; [11] If by any means I might attain unto the resurrection of the dead. [12] Not as though I had already attained, either were already perfect: but I follow after, if that I may apprehend that for which also I am apprehended of Christ Jesus. [13] Brethren, I count not myself to have apprehended: but this one thing I do, forgetting those things which are behind, and reaching forth unto those things which are before, [14] I press toward the mark for the prize of the high calling of God in Christ Jesus. [15] Let us therefore, as many as be perfect, be thus minded: and if in any thing ye be otherwise minded, God shall reveal even this unto you."

Contrary to the lies that have corrupted many of God's people, following Christ means to seek first the Kingdom of God and His righteousness! There is nothing second. If you find this repulsive to the life you want for yourself, then check out your salvation, whether you be of the faith. Perhaps you are one in the parable that thought you knew Him, but clearly, He did not know you.

(Matthew 7:23) KJV
"And then will I profess unto them, I never knew you: depart from me, ye that work iniquity."

(2 Corinthians 13:5) KJV
"Examine yourselves, whether ye be in the faith; prove your own selves. Know ye not your own selves, how that Jesus Christ is in you, except ye be reprobates?"

Besides all this, for me, to live is Christ and to die is gain!

(Philippians 1:21) KJV
"For to me to live is Christ, and to die is gain."

Obedience Because of Love

Though it should be obvious, it's not. In the simplicity of it, Jesus explained it in one sentence:

(John 14:21) KJV
"He that hath my commandments, and keepnet them, he it is that loveth me: and he that loveth me shall be loved of my Father, and I will love him, and will manifest myself to him."

Of all the explanations that we as human beings give to describe how much we love Jesus, they cannot replace His standard of what it means to love Him.

Keeping His commandments is the only gateway of being loved by the Father and the Son and the assurance of Him manifesting Himself to you. It is the only evidence that will meet the required kingdom of God's standard to enter into an intimate relationship with God and His Son Jesus Christ. PERIOD.

I can already hear a few workarounds to this truth which is rooted in a well-crafted argument. Just keep one thing in mind about well-crafted arguments; anytime it nullifies one jot or tittle of scripture, it is a false doctrine. The falsehood should be especially apparent when it erodes away obeying

Jesus – Savior, and Lord! Furthermore, the immediate result of disobedience is sin, and sin brings forth death when it is finished. Besides this, why seek ways to sin when the life He wants to give us is filled with joy and peace in the Holy Ghost.

(1 John 3:9-10) KJV
"Whosoever is born of God doth not commit sin; for his seed remaineth in him: and he cannot sin, because he is born of God. [10] In this the children of God are manifest, and the children of the devil: whosoever doeth not righteousness is not of God, neither he that loveth not his brother."

As you strive to discover the Will of God, obedience by love will be the constant that brings you ever closer to a clearer vision of His Will for your life. His power working through you to perform it will become manifest daily. Nothing will nor can replace obedience because it brings delight to the Father and is the very act of doing His Will. However, obedience is not just where you start will start, but it is also where you end.

We often misconstrue obedience because we think it has to do with something we'd instead not want to do. Or we think we are giving up control of our will in a way that does not benefit us. It does appear that way, but it is actually not true. If you believe the nature of God is good and that He loves you, then anything He asks of you is good. Therefore, to obey a good and loving Father has to have profound benefits that far exceed what we can even think or imagine.

Furthermore, to disobey is harming us. The Lord is not trying to keep good things from us; instead, He desires to keep that which does not benefit us from affecting our lives. If our natural father expects us to obey him and we believe that what he has asked us to do is good, how much more, our heavenly Father?

(Hebrews 12:9-10) KJV
"Furthermore, we have had fathers of our flesh which corrected us, and we gave them reverence: shall we not much rather be in subjection unto the Father of spirits, and live? [10] For they verily for a few days chastened us after their own pleasure; but he for our profit, that we might be partakers of his holiness."

However, another layer to the obedience that we fail to realize plays a vital role in our spiritual life now and especially our eternal life to come. It is so powerful that this is where the enemy realizes the danger of letting you flow in a place of obedience to God's written Word and His Spirit's leading. He knows the influence, favor, and power with God you obtain when you obey Him. What that means to Satan is that he is obstructed from distracting and hindering you from being in a relevant space with God moment by moment. Do you realize how valuable your obedience is?

(1 Samuel 15:22) KJV
"And Samuel said, Hath the LORD as great delight in burnt offerings and sacrifices, as in obeying the voice of the LORD? Behold, to obey is better than sacrifice, and to hearken than the fat of rams."

Anything that we do for God, follows obedience. In other words, giving money, serving in the church, feeding the hungry, and clothing the poor, are as good as me being obedient to the written and revealed Will of God in a personal and intimate way. This is where our conscience comes in because that is a space within us that only God owns. We cannot shut it down or shut it up (unless of course, we are reprobates).

(1 John 3:19-22) KJV
"And hereby we know that we are of the truth, and shall assure our hearts before him. [20] For if our heart condemn us, God is greater than our heart, and knoweth all things. [21] Beloved, if our heart condemn us not, then have we confidence toward God. [22] And whatsoever we ask, we receive of him, because we keep his commandments, and do those things that are pleasing in his sight."

Obedience is the benchmark of spiritual maturity. It is the very place that God takes painstaking time measured in decades to get us to live and abide at. We traverse countless experiences of failures to finally arrive at this joyous place of communion, and we cherish and protect it. We witnessed this undisturbed connection with the Father when Jesus declared that He "always" did things that pleased His Father.

(John 8:29) KJV
[29] "And he that sent me is with me: the Father hath not left me alone; for I do always those things that please him."

After nearly 25 years, Abraham was blessed with Isaac to only be asked to sacrifice him. What did Abraham do? He said nothing to Sarah but rose up early the following day and left. He recalled telling Sarah that God would give them a son. After failed attempts, Sarah turned to tradition, and even though God never suggested this as an option, Abraham yielded to her voice. Ishmael through Haggar was the result. This time, however, he knew Sarah would not understand what God had asked of him. Nor was it for her to understand. It was for him to obey God! How often we fail when we attempt to persuade others of what God has told us to do. Anything that God tells us to do is an invitation to worship, and the highest form of worship is **OBEDIENCE!**

(Genesis 22:1-3) KJV
"And it came to pass after these things, that God did tempt Abraham, and said unto him, Abraham: and he said, Behold, here I am. [2] And he said, Take now thy son, thine only son Isaac, whom thou lovest, and get thee into the land of Moriah; and offer him there for a burnt offering upon one of the mountains which I will tell thee of. [3] And Abraham rose up early in the morning, and saddled his ass, and took two of his young men with him, and Isaac his son, and clave the wood for the burnt offering, and rose up, and went unto the place of which God had told him."

Notice how God understood that Abraham loved Isaac. "Whom thou lovest". God always asks you to give Him the thing that you love. He demands those projects, those pleasures, and especially the souls of those dear to us. I fear that many Christians are failing to discover God's Will for them because they have chosen the will of another. They have drawn a line in the sand for GOD not to cross because it would cost them *whom thou lovest*. After decades of experiencing the faithfulness of God, Abraham finally had come to realize that anything he had was because of God and for God – and that included Isaac. He had resolved in his heart of hearts that it wasn't about Isaac; it was about God. He would never again allow fear and pride to distract him from obeying God. For him, it was simple – "let's go, Isaac, we're going to worship! I can imagine how excited Abraham was because he had seen the faithfulness of God over the years and how patient He had been with him. Abraham was so ready to worship because he knew that he had discovered the origin of His faith – it was to please God in whatever God had asked of him.

(Genesis 22:4-6) KJV
"Then on the third day, Abraham lifted up his eyes and saw the place afar off. [5] And Abraham said unto his young men, Abide ye here with the ass; and I and the lad will go yonder and worship, and come again to you. [6] And Abraham took the wood of the burnt offering, and laid it upon Isaac his son; and he took the fire in his hand, and a knife; and they went both of them together."

Abraham resolved that this was a promise that God had made and if it meant He had to raise Isaac up from the dead, then He would. Obedience means leaving 100% of the results to God.

(Hebrews 11:17-19) KJV
"By faith Abraham, when he was tried, offered up Isaac: and he that had received the promises offered up his only begotten son, [18] Of whom it was said, That in Isaac shall thy seed be called: [19] Accounting that God was able to raise him up, even from the dead; from whence also he received him in a figure."

This wasn't the first time Abraham was tried. However, he knew this to be the height of his walk with God, and therefore, it would be a determining factor in where things would go from here. Good intentions and assumptions would not work. It had to become official. God is no respecter of persons, which means both you and I will be tried. Until we officially pass those milestone tests in our lives, we remain where we are. The only way to be permitted to transition to the next place of faith is to obey the voice of your loving Heavenly Father right where you stand! The result of Abrahams's obedience enshrined him throughout eternity as a man who would not withhold anything from God!

(Genesis 22:10-11, 13-18) KJV
"And Abraham stretched forth his hand and took the knife to slay his son. [11] And the angel of the LORD called unto him out of heaven, and said, Abraham, Abraham: and he said, Here am I. [13] And Abraham lifted up his eyes, and looked, and behold behind him a ram caught in a thicket by his horns: and Abraham went and took the ram, and offered him up for a burnt offering in the stead of his son. [14] And Abraham called the name of that place Jehovah-Jireh: as it is said to this day,

In the mount of the LORD it shall be seen. [15] And the angel of the LORD called unto Abraham out of heaven the second time, [16] And said, By myself have I sworn, saith the LORD, for because thou hast done this thing, and hast not withheld thy son, thine only son: [17] That in blessing I will bless thee, and in multiplying I will multiply thy seed as the stars of the heaven, and as the sand which is upon the seashore; and thy seed shall possess the gate of his enemies; [18] And in thy seed shall all the nations of the earth be blessed; because thou hast obeyed my voice."

Verses are being written right now about you that all the heavenly host and the innumerable company of believers will one day read. What will it say? If you obey His voice, it will be an eternal testimony that will be uttered throughout the new heaven and new earth. We each have an altar, a knife, and He will provide the sacrifice. Only fear God, and He will keep that which He has promised. If it is not His Will, let it die, and that which is - will come to life – even if it must die.

Suffering

(Colossians 1:23-25) KJV
"If ye continue in the faith grounded and settled, and be not moved away from the hope of the gospel, which ye have heard, and which was preached to every creature which is under heaven; whereof I Paul am made a minister; [24] Who now rejoice in my sufferings for you, and fill up that which is behind of the afflictions of Christ in my flesh for his body's sake, which is the church: [25] Whereof I am made a minister, according to the dispensation of God which is given to me for you, to fulfil the word of God;"

(1 Peter 4:12-13) KJV
[12] "Beloved, think it not strange concerning the fiery trial which is to try you, as though some strange thing happened unto you: [13] But rejoice, inasmuch as ye are partakers of Christ's sufferings; that, when his glory shall be revealed, ye may be glad also with exceeding joy."

When you take the journey that God has created you to experience, your mind and spirit have been touched by the divine. You have received an impartation from heaven. This world loses its luster, and the appeal of the flesh does not satisfy any longer. Jesus becomes the Son of God to you in a personal and intimate way. He is not merely a Bible character or a hero figure that saves you from your sins and that's it. He is in you and speaks to you, and the Father has also made His abode with you.

In suffering, we must do so with rejoicing! We have been given the privilege of partaking in His suffering that will manifest in the glory yet to be revealed! To the extent that we suffer will be the measure of the extent of the glory!

When this happens, you embrace every aspect of the journey God has ordained for you. Suffering is a part of this, and you see it as a glorious honor because it brings with it more than can be understood or even expressed. Again, however, this is the suffering that has to do with pursuing His Will. There is suffering for disobedience, unwise decisions, and so forth. Yet, mysteriously, God even uses these experiences for our good - if we love Him.

(Romans 8:28) KJV
"And we know that all things work together for good to them that love God, to them who are the called according to his purpose."

Carefully reading the verses following this, however, my mind cannot grasp this truth. In the sovereignty of God, He had already made provision for my struggles, which is so beautiful! It is then I realize IF God is for me who can be against me!

(Romans 8:27, 29-31) KJV
[29] "For whom he did foreknow, he also did predestinate to be conformed to the image of his Son, that he might be the firstborn among many brethren. [30] Moreover whom he did predestinate, them he also called: and whom he called, them he also justified: and whom he justified, them he also glorified. [31] What shall we then say to these things? If God be for us, who can be against us?"

Therefore, you can have confidence in your sufferings. God "foreknew" you! That means He already knew your failures and the journey you would have to take to be conformed to the image of His Son[2]. But there is more! When He called you, He justified you, and then He glorified you! When you grasp this daily, there is no way you can resist the

---

2   Conformed in the sense of his likeness not in terms of salvation which is a free gift according to grace by faith. We cannot earn our salvation whatsoever. However, as we mature in this salvation that we have received, we are called upon to conform our lives to that of Jesus.

Journey By Faith

pursuit of such a lover! How can you not want to take this eternal journey?

Suffering is a gateway to glory not only in the life to come but even in this life. Paul understood this, and so do many others. The heroes of the faith in (Hebrews 11) knew it so well that they didn't want deliverance from their sufferings so that they might experience a better resurrection! Imagine that! They wanted to die at the mouths of lions because they had seen the glorious rewards that awaited them by faith.

(1 Peter 3:14) KJV
[14] "But and if ye suffer for righteousness sake, happy are ye: and be not afraid of their terror, neither be troubled;"

(1 Peter 4:1-2) KJV
"Forasmuch then as Christ hath suffered for us in the flesh, arm yourselves likewise with the same mind: for he that hath suffered in the flesh hath ceased from sin; [2] That he no longer should live the rest of his time in the flesh to the lusts of men, but to the will of God."

Another aspect of suffering that those who would be mature in Christ must confront and overcome, is sin. Sin is to miss the mark by being held as a prisoner to your fallen nature. Only through Christ can this fallen nature be rendered dead. Through Christ's death, I died, and therefore, through Christ's resurrection, I live. When we accept His death for our death and His life as our life, we begin living this transformation daily. Through our journey, we come to learn that only through suffering can I cease from sin.

To be clearer, when I say suffering, I am not by any means suggesting that we can obtain this position in Christ by works or self-will efforts. No! We are by grace complete in Christ through faith alone. The suffering that I speak of is that of "working out your own salvation in fear and trembling." It is resisting the devil, humbling yourself under the mighty hand of God, bringing your body into subjection, and making no provisions for the flesh. There is a suffering in all of this.

(Philippians 2:12) KJV
"Wherefore, my beloved, as ye have always obeyed, not as in my presence only, but now much more in my absence, work out your own salvation with fear and trembling."

(James 4:6-7) KJV
"But he giveth more grace. Wherefore he saith, God resisteth the proud, but giveth grace unto the humble. [7] Submit yourselves therefore to God. Resist the devil, and he will flee from you."

(1 Corinthians 9:27) KJV
"But I keep under my body, and bring it into subjection: lest that by any means, when I have preached to others, I myself should be a castaway."

(Romans 13:14) KJV
"But put ye on the Lord Jesus Christ, and make not provision for the flesh, to fulfil the lusts thereof."

Journey By Faith

When you yield to your renewed spirit, the flesh itself will suffer because its nature is very much still there though dead. Yes, it is there but dead, and if you feed it, it will drag you back to death and separate you from the love of Christ. Sin separates. If you live after the flesh, you will die!

(Romans 8:13) KJV
"For if ye live after the flesh, ye shall die: but if ye through the Spirit do mortify the deeds of the body, ye shall live."

Many Christians struggle with the flesh because they have not connected their body with their confession. They have been led to believe that they can live after the flesh and still experience a relationship with Christ and even eternal life. Suppose we believe that we can LIVE after the flesh (as a lifestyle) and yet be in a vibrant, joyous, fruitful relationship with Christ. In that case, we deceive ourselves because Christ is not the minister of sin. I could go on a biblical and worthwhile discussion about this, but I won't. Suffice to say:

(Galatians 2:17) KJV
"But if, while we seek to be justified by Christ, we ourselves also are found sinners, is therefore Christ the minister of sin? God forbid."

Now that we understand the purpose of suffering, expect it on your journey by faith, and recognize it as the gateway to discovering and then fulfilling God's will for your life. Equip yourself with the power of God's Word to arrest the flesh and bring it under the cross of Calvary. Know that we have not resisted to that of blood striving against sin and therefore we need not be weary or faint in our minds!

(Hebrews 12:3-4) KJV
"For consider him that endured such contradiction of sinners against himself, lest ye be wearied and faint in your minds. [4] Ye have not yet resisted unto blood, striving against sin."

Finally, in suffering, we are not alone. We can commit ourselves to Him, knowing that we are safe in any trial we face. We must eradicate any thinking in our minds that is contrary to God being a faithful Creator. If we don't, we will always succumb to a type of fear that tells us we will suffer needlessly and in vain. It is a lie forged in the pit of hell to keep you from trusting God more and more. As you strive to discover and fulfill God's Will through your journey by faith, you will be faced with this temptation time and time again. Don't waste time trying to persuade yourself, rather, rebuke the devil with "it is written" and read this to him.

(1 Peter 4:19) KJV
[19] "Wherefore let them that suffer according to the will of God commit the keeping of their souls to him in well doing, as unto a faithful Creator."

In the faithfulness of God, He has a plan in your suffering and also a timeline. When it is accomplished, He will settle you, establish you, and then strengthen you afresh!

When that happens, it will be in part determined by your own resolve to trust Him and humble yourself to Him by enduring and embracing the cross He has for you. The very thing you are suffering through is custom-made for your purpose. If you don't accept this, you will never mature and always resolve to complain and miss the divine objective that can only be received by faith through your journey.

(1 Peter 5:10) KJV
[10] "But the God of all grace, who hath called us unto his eternal glory by Christ Jesus, after that ye have suffered a while, make you perfect, establish, strengthen, settle you."

Marriage and Faith

Next to your relationship with Jesus and the Father, no other will have a more influential impact on your life than marriage. It will either bring a refreshing revelation of Christ and His Bride or create a stronghold of conflict that you'll have to spend most of your life trying to resolve. This is difficult while also trying to discover and fulfill God's Will. It is the sweetest or the bitterest. Most of our lives are spent grappling with the reality of marriage. Millions of books, articles, opinions, workshops and counseling sessions have offered insights into two human beings' mysterious union. It is a never-ending reality of life. In the midst of this, we are baffled by the reality of marriage difficulties and, sad to say, failures. I know this to be true in a personal way. I was married for 29 years, and we raised four children together. It ended because of one primary reason: FAITH. Amid the trials, the counseling, and the resolves, it always circled back to that one element: FAITH. We were both Christians and loved the Lord and each other. [QR CODE]

Though heartbroken, I resolved to become better and not bitter. It was this experience that drove me deeper in my faith in God. I knew that God knew my heart and that I would not, nor could I forsake my faith and call for anything or anyone. First, however, I had to accept that I could not represent another person's faith – even my wife's. Nor could I deny my faith for to do so would be to deny Christ.

I share this with you not to cast blame or justify anything because we all have fallen short of God's glory. I reflect on this to focus on one principle that will be the force of a good marriage or a bad one: FAITH. This applies to Christians who profess Christ as much as it involves not marrying an unbeliever. Many believe that the only thing that matters is that they are Christian. Being unequally yoked goes beyond putting faith in Christ for salvation; it also applies to placing faith in Christ for His Will to be done in your lives through that marriage. Will it enhance it or hinder it?

Being Single

At the outset, it is challenging to discover single men or women who are living their faith through a real-life journey with knowledge of their purpose. Today's culture has taken so many Christian singles hostage into a vice-like grip of making it about themselves, pleasurable things, and just all about this life. If you have not resolved to pursue the high calling of God, there are plenty of low calling singles out there. However, suppose you are in pursuit of your journey by faith, in that case, your only hope is to give yourself entirely to God's Will and His Kingdom without distraction while seeking Him only for that person in your life. This removes the burden off you and allows you to be single in the heart in serving the Lord. It has, over time, become the only option for me.

I don't recommend dating apps just because it makes it easy to find someone supposedly. Of course, if the Lord quickens you to do so, Amen. Bear in mind that the amount of time it takes to shuffle through the content; you could have been that further along in discovering and fulfilling God's Will. Likewise, a relationship that comes into your life through your own pursuits is less likely to involve the perfect Will of God. Another factor is that it preoccupies the emotions that can take you up and down. This can and will cause your spirit to find it challenging to cultivate a steadfastness with God for your own spiritual health.

If you are single, the best position you can place yourself in to discover who that person could be (if at all) is to know and fulfill your purpose. Then, as you discover and fulfill God's Will as a lifestyle, you are attuned to a level of faith in God that assures you that He knows the desires of your heart.

Seeking first His kingdom and His righteousness assures you that all things will be added unto you, including that wife or husband moving in the same realm of faith that you are. The yoke that binds to a spouse aligned with you is that you both have a living faith, an experienced faith, and live a fulfilled life of faith. This is not to suggest that even then, marriage will not have its challenges. However, if being single, you cannot obtain this level of clarity; you certainly won't do so being married. So now you have two people who are now striving to become one are unsure of who they are as individuals! Don't go there.

Your completeness is not found in marriage; first, it is found in Christ. Many marriages were doomed for failure because they were looking to be complete with someone else. Marriage can be summed up in one word: SERVANT! We have been called to serve that person as we would want to be served.

Single Men

You need to understand a fundamental principle as a single

man: A woman was not made to make you whole or give you purpose. Nor is she there for you to make a "happy wife, so you can have a happy life", really? Your identity is in Christ, and it will be from Him that you obtain your purpose and then begin to live in it without the "need" to be married. Take your journey and discover who you are as a person and as a man. Treasure your aloneness and solitude. As I travel in my RV throughout America, it has been the richest part of my life to wake up and just be. The joy I've had to lay in my bed and allow God to flood my mind and heart with His voice, and reflect on the scriptures, and to obtain the instructions that He has for me for the day is divine. If you don't know your purpose and prove it by living it, how can you possibly know if the woman would even qualify to be the helpmeet you will need? Too many men settle for less and, therefore, marry a face that makes a good companion but turns out to be a terrible helpmeet.

As a man, you need time to discover yourself and process. Allow the Lord to unveil your scars, insecurities, and fears. Let Him heal you and give you a knowing that will take you throughout your life. I know this to be true. After my divorce, I needed to replace that void (so I thought). So, I went through several different relationships that I thought had the potential to become serious. The deeper I got into the relationship, the more I realized my own lack of trusting God with that need in my life. I was compromising myself with relationships that were not intense in the faith as I was. That doesn't mean they were not nice or didn't love the Lord. It was just obvious that our faith was not equally yoked. Many times, I would compensate for them so that it would possibly work. That is a bad decision. If a woman or man does not want to work out their own salvation and pursue the things of God on their own, they will only resent you for trying to get them to do it.

Single Women

In today's culture, being a woman is immensely challenging. So many ideas have forced themselves upon the identity of being a woman that what God has to say about you has become comical, or even worse. Many think it is repulsive to root your womanhood in the identity of the one who made you. Navigating this subject is challenging because most Christians have been conditioned by the world's narrative. As a result, we have failed to have our minds transformed and renewed. Therefore, when we hear the truth, we react. I know this book is about Faith, but for faith to be relevant, it has to spring forth from an identity rooted in truth, and tht truth is CHRIST. If you attempt to apply faith to a twisted and worldly narrative, it will cease to flow from your identity in Christ.

Having said that, a woman has been elevated to a position unique to her created purpose. She is likened to the Body of Christ and to be loved as such! Christ came to establish the woman as one who would be enabled to receive the love of a husband as Christ loves the Church and to submit to that love as the Church would to Christ. But what does that mean when it comes to living life by faith? In simple terms, it provides you an easy yoke and a light burden. It also casts off the requirements of a society that is desperate to force you into conformity of identity that places you at variance with the man instead of in harmony with him. Society's arguments are centered on being equal with something created and not unique by the Creator! The tragedy about this entire narrative is that it never satisfies. There is no end to it because it's false from the start.

In your journey by faith as a single woman, I encourage you to fiercely reject and resist any narrative void of the intimate love that Christ has for you. The revelation of who you are in Him is yours to discover.

Your journey is with Him and for Him. In being single, you have the time and the freedom to discover Him as Father, as Friend, and as One who can and will satisfy you beyond that of any man. When this satisfaction is a living part of your daily life, you will have the experience of this love to measure any man who comes into your life. You will see beyond the natural and discern if he comes to love you as Christ would to the Church or to love you from his own lack of identity.

There is no way I can do this subject justice in this small section, and for sure, I did not get it all right. So, I simply pray you to come to grips with one principle: Obtain the fullness of who God created you to be while you are single, and leave becoming ONE to God. He knows the desires of your heart, and in His sovereignty through your journey by faith you will be discovered and pursued by the man who has a faith that is equally yoked with yours in Christ.

Chapter Four

Discovering the Will of God

(Philippians 3:12-16) KJV
"Not as though I had already attained, either were already perfect: but I follow after, if that I may apprehend that for which also I am apprehended of Christ Jesus."

It should give us peace knowing that none of us have 'already attained' the fullness of what God has created us for. It reveals in such simple words that God doesn't expect us, nor does He allow us to have the complete revelation of our creation. To do so would element the need for faith altogether. To place this "attaining" into context, I encourage you to read the scriptures above this, starting at verse 8. It sets the bar for what that means, from knowing the excellency of the knowledge of Christ, suffering for Christ, avoiding my own self-righteousness, and ultimately experiencing the resurrection.

Journey By Faith

The portion I care to focus on is to apprehend what He apprehended of us and at what cost Paul emphasizes he is willing to pay.

I follow after...

Regardless of where you start or where you end, you have to resolve to follow after Christ. The first step in discovering the Will of God for your life is to follow after Christ. By now, you should know I'm not speaking of religious works. I refer to an intimate, deliberate moment by moment of following Jesus with an intensity that reveals your desire for Him. This is compounded by your relationship with the Father because it is the Father whose Will you do. You can only follow one person, one objective, and one passion at a time. This is not a passive hobby. It becomes your life, and you are doing so with a purpose – to apprehend! The amplified version puts it this way:

... but I {actively} press on so that I may take hold of that [perfection] for which Christ Jesus took hold of me and made me His own.

"Actively." To be active is to be intentional, consistent, and therefore possess a resolve that this is the ONE thing you are pursuing in your life with expectations of the life to come. This is a world apart from the traditional and religious entrapment that many Christians live in today. In fact, many who claim they are Christians prove they are not when the fruit is inspected. They are following another Jesus and another Gospel altogether (Galatians 1:6.7).

Statistics say that as many as 70-90% of Americans will tell you they are "Christian." However, when you ask people to define what a Christian is, it becomes apparent that most are totally misled as to what it means to be a Christian. The most common answer, in my observation, is that they believe that Jesus is the Son of God, is a good person, and attends church regularly. The devils believe that Jesus is the Son of God too, and they tremble at His name. This deception lies in the fact that most don't believe one's confession will be evident in the fruit they bear. This is where many have been deceived. They have a form of godliness but deny the power of it. They say, "Lord, Lord," but do not what He says. When such individuals stand before the Lord, they will be in utter disbelief when He tells them,

(Luke 13:27) KJV
[27] "But he shall say, I tell you, I know you not whence ye are; depart from me, all ye workers of iniquity."

Forgetting Those Things...

[13] "Brethren, I count not myself to have apprehended: but this one thing I do, forgetting those things which are behind, and reaching forth unto those things which are before,"

Whether it is yourself, other people, the devil, or a combination of them all, attempts to keep you stagnant are most effective in keeping you in a state of the past. This scripture gives you the authority to literally nullify any demon or human being who seeks to hold you as a prisoner to your yesterday. Regardless of what it might look like or how horrible it could be, the scripture gives us the authority to forget about it! When you have resolved to discover God's Will, forgetting will become a significant decision you learn to implement in your daily life.

However, this is not to be used carelessly, nor does it ignore other scriptural standards where applicable. Sin, for example, should not be justified by saying, "Well, I'll just forget about it!" Sin needs to be confessed and repented with heartfelt soberness (1 John 1:9). This basis for this scripture is to allow us total freedom to discover who we are in Christ. While in this life, we will have inconsistencies, setbacks, distractions, and so on. However, because of the completed work of Christ, as often as I need to, without compromising scriptural integrity, I can just "forget about it."

While I realize the memory of the past will also linger in our minds, its effects need not hinder our journey in discovery. Therefore, when tempted by the past, we can affirm our positional right with Christ to say, "I will forget this issue that has been covered by Christ and press toward the mark!"

Press Toward the Mark

Philippians 3:14 (KJV)
"I press toward the mark for the prize of the high calling of God in Christ Jesus."
[14] (AMP) "I press on toward the goal to win the [heavenly] prize of the upward call of God in Christ Jesus."

When you are pressing toward the mark, you can't afford to be distracted, and this is why this divine right to forget is so critical in your journey of discovering the Will of God for your life. If you've ever pressed weights on a bench press, you realize the focus it takes to leave the weight on the bar. In fact, you can't even talk while you are pressing because you are breathing! When you have purposed to press toward the mark of the HIGH calling of God, it demands your sole focus. To press into something means you have the resolve to obtain what you are hoping for. You also believe that it is worth it to press towards a specific mark with a prize associated with it. Finally, when it is the high calling of "GOD" in Christ Jesus, nothing could be more specifically related to your purpose than that which you are pursuing.

We need to strive to see what God sees in our journey of faith. He is pleased with us even as He was with the Son when He did His Will. How do you feel when you see your child in harmony with what you require of them? You are proud of their obedience and attention to what you expect of them. Even so, your Heavenly Father is of you! In the sight of God, it is lovely beyond description when you are pressing after the High Calling that He created you for.

(Matthew 3:17) KJV
"And lo a voice from heaven, saying, This is my beloved Son, in whom I am well pleased."

Be Thus Minded

Philippians 3:15 KJV
Let us therefore, as many as be perfect, be thus minded: and if in any thing ye be otherwise minded, God shall reveal even this unto you.

Discovering the Will of God requires a mindset that is biblically rooted in your identity in Christ. It is the position that Christ has placed you in by His own righteousness and perfect sacrifice. His death raised you up to newness of life by destroying your old man (Romans 6:4-6), granted you access to eternal life (John 6:40), quickened you who were dead in transgressions, and given you to be seated with Christ in heavenly places (Ephesians 2:1-6)! This spiritual position is not a matter of persuasion through mind games; it is an eternal and legal fact that you must appropriate by faith and declare it to yourself and others on the earth and in the heavenly. This is where we make known the manifold wisdom of God with a resolve that will not be shaken.

(Ephesians 3:9-12) KJV
"And to make all men see what is the fellowship of the mystery, which from the beginning of the world hath been hid in God, who created all things by Jesus Christ: [10] To the intent that now unto the principalities and powers in heavenly places might be known by the church the manifold wisdom of God, [11] According to the eternal purpose which he purposed in Christ Jesus our Lord [12] In whom we have boldness and access with confidence by the faith of him."

Notice how verse 11 qualifies this by establishing that it is according to the eternal purpose which HE (GOD) purposed in Christ Jesus our Lord!

What is the problem with God's people? Why are we so sheepish when it comes to taking hold of the promises of God in Christ and becoming that vessel that God has ordained before the foundations of the world for us to be? All we need do is to walk where we have attained and keep walking, and we will discover the Will of God unfolding around us moment by moment with signs and wonders following! If nothing can separate us from His love and no weapon formed against us can prosper, and He will meet our needs according to His riches in glory, while having confidence that we are asking in line with His Will, it is clear that the issue lies with us.

Journey By Faith

[16] "Nevertheless, whereto we have already attained, let us walk by the same rule, let us mind the same thing."

I love the word "nevertheless." It gives us clarity of mind and removes the need to be confused about anything. When you accept the fact that God has ordered the steps of a righteous man, you learn to accept you are where He wants you to be. In other words, "just flow" where God has brought you. Stay honest with where you have arrived, and God will keep bringing you to where He is ordained you be.

At this very moment, I'm at an RV park writing this book. I had planned to be in New Orleans sharing the gospel in the French Quarter. However, in the providence of God, He redirected my feet to be here. It happened in a totally unexpected way. I was at the cleaners picking up my clothes, and the owner noticed my RV and said, we'll roll with you! Then he told me where they were going on the weekend. I immediately looked it up on google maps and called to get some more information. In my conversation with the owner, I asked if they provided any entertainment for the people, and he said he hasn't since COVID. I told him what I did with poetry and my drum, and he immediately asked how much I usually charge. I told him $200, he said can we do $150, and I'll give you a spot to park your RV. I said, " Deal!" Not only did he give me a spot for my RV, but he feed me one of the best steaks I've ever had on day one and the freshest crab legs on the next day! As I prepared to leave on Monday, it rained all day Sunday; as a result, the ground was soaked. To drive on this would not be wise. I told him, and he said, no problem, no one needs that spot until May 18, so take your time. That was about 8 days from then! The thought had just run through my mind how nice it would be to stay here, work on my books, and edit online course videos. Well, God had just precisely provided that in allowing me to extend my stay.

However, while all of this was indeed a blessing, it would come full circle when I heard the news of what happened in New Orleans. A tornado had swept through the city, and there was damage everywhere! All I could do was worship God! He spared me from possible harm and damage to my RV, blessed me with income, not including the offerings I received. Feed me steak and crab gave me time to just rest and reflect while focusing on the writing of this book! That's just how faithful He is and desires to be every day of our lives. So if you're ever near Moss Point, Mississippi, be sure to look up Presley's Outing! It is family friendly, affordable and again the food is great. Tell Mr. Presley I sent you!

Just flow. Trust. Worship. Take no thought for your life. It is in this attitude of obedience that the Will of God becomes more apparent, and God will not allow you to trust in your emotions or opinions but will support His direction with signs and wonders following, and especially the fruit!

Hear His voice and simply begin to do as He reveals to you in your mind and in your spirit.

The Evidence

I am overwhelmed with wonder in living a lifestyle of faith! There is never a dull moment or lack of opportunity to experience God especially having the joy of witnessing the fruit of righteousness coming forth in my life. It is how God confirms His Will while assuring me that I am on the right path. The purest witness is that of peace that surpasses all understanding as I remain steadfast in prayer, supplication, and thanksgiving on my journey of faith.

(Philippians 4:6-7) KJV
"Be careful for nothing; but in every thing by prayer and supplication with thanksgiving let your requests be made known unto God. [7] And the peace of God, which passeth all understanding, shall keep your hearts and minds through Christ Jesus."

I have discovered that this peace is not the peace that the world gives. The world's method of peace originates from creation. Anything that touches you from the outside, whether food, things, sex, pleasure, money, and the like is of the world. God's peace is a result of **WHO** is on the inside of you, and the peace is personal – direct from the CREATOR, which means it is relevant to who you are, where you are, and the journey ahead of you. His peace is not temperamental or determined by circumstances or even your emotional state of being. In fact, He is PEACE Himself. One of His names is Prince of Peace! Too many people attempt to get their emotions settled to experience peace instead of getting their hearts right with the Prince of Peace!

(John 14:27) KJV
"Peace I leave with you, my peace I give unto you: not as the world giveth, give I unto you. Let not your heart be troubled, neither let it be afraid."

When you are on the journey of discovering God's Will with a sincere and repentive heart, His peace is immediate. There is no performance required, no explanation needed to be given, or church service to attend. In submitting to the King of kings and the Lord of lords, you initiate a divine realm of overruling. This means all of your circumstances in every sphere of life: financial, relational, emotional, physical, and even political, come under His rule. As you remain submitted to His Will, He will cause all things to work together for your good. However, you have to submit yourself genuinely and do so with a humble heart. Don't think for one second you can fool God. So many people think they can! You would be surprised at the result! I've had my share of holding back, and He smiles and just waits for me to come straight with Him. He is truly loving, kind, and patient.

(1 Peter 5:6-8) KJV
"Humble yourselves therefore under the mighty hand of God, that he may exalt you in due time: [7] Casting all your care upon him; for he careth for you. [8] Be sober, be vigilant; because your adversary the devil, as a roaring lion, walketh about, seeking whom he may devour:"

It is in this humility that you find protection from yourself and from your adversary, the devil. He is vehemently opposed to you discovering the Will of God. Let me explain why.

Your adversary, the devil

To understand to even a small degree the darker than dark (of what we know dark to be) hatred that the devil has of you, you need to understand who he was before he became Satan. He was called Lucifer, the son of the morning!

(Isaiah 14:11-16) KJV
"Thy pomp is brought down to the grave, and the noise of thy viols: the worm is spread under thee, and the worms cover thee. [12] How art thou fallen from heaven, O Lucifer, son of the morning! how art thou cut down to the ground, which didst weaken the nations! [13] For thou hast said in thine heart, I will ascend into heaven, I will exalt my throne above the stars of God: I will sit also upon the mount of the congregation, in the sides of the north: [14] I will ascend above the heights of the clouds; I will be like the most High. [15] Yet thou shalt be brought down to hell, to the sides of the pit. [16] They that see thee shall narrowly look upon thee, and consider thee, saying, Is this the man that made the earth to tremble, that did shake kingdom:"

You need to read this carefully. This is your adversary! Look at all he had and what he lost. Notice his outcome and the shock the nations will have when they realize who he really was that made the earth tremble. He was nothing! When we come to understand just a fraction of who we are in Christ, we come to also realize the authority He has given us over the devil. However, that authority is released upon us as we are humbled to Him and His Will. The danger is when we presumptuously think that just because we can say the name of "Jesus," that we have the authority of Jesus.

The reality of the Will of God being revealed is indeed mysterious, divine, and constant. You will arrive moment by moment at the Will of God because the Will of God is alive! It is transcending both time and space. It is a real relationship that continues to grow into a living expression of who God made you be. We are His workmanship created to bring forth good works which has been ordained by Him and that glorifies Him in a way nothing else can.

(Ephesians 2:10) KJV
"For we are his workmanship, created in Christ Jesus unto good works, which God hath before ordained that we should walk in them."

Be Filled with All the Fulness of God and Go Forth!

(Ephesians 3:11-12,16,21) KJV
"According to the eternal purpose which he purposed in Christ Jesus our

Lord: [12] In whom we have boldness and access with confidence by the faith of him. [16] That he would grant you, according to the riches of his glory, to be strengthened with might by his Spirit in the inner man; [17] That Christ may dwell in your hearts by faith; that ye, being rooted and grounded in love, [18] May be able to comprehend with all saints what is the breadth, and length, and depth, and height; [19] And to know the love of Christ, which passeth knowledge, that ye might be filled with all the fulness of God. [20] Now unto him that is able to do exceeding abundantly above all that we ask or think, according to the power that worketh in us, [21] Unto him be glory in the church by Christ Jesus throughout all ages, world without end. Amen."

Reread it one more time.

Now ask God for a Rhema word of revelation on how this applies to you.

I could write another chapter just on this alone! The Will of God for you is not of you or of this world. It is according to HIS eternal purpose, which HE purposed in Christ! The discovery of it is found in discovering Christ and Who He is as Savior and Lord to YOU! The boldness given to us is IN HIM and the faith to access all that He has for us. This faith is not of you; it is of HIM! Don't confuse faith with self-willed determination or effort. The Will of God blossoms within you as you allow Christ to dwell in your heart by "faith." In childlike faith, let your soul be rooted and grounded in love.

Love is the cornerstone of discovering God's Will because God is love, and it also proves to be one of the most telling signs that you are moving in harmony with heaven because you love people.

As you grasp these truths, allow God's Spirit to dwell in you richly that you may know what the hope of His calling is. I am confident that the discovery of God's Will shall become evident more and more, and you will abound in fulfilling it moment by moment with joy unspeakable and full of glory! Be at peace that you may be able to pierce into the riches of the glory of His inheritance for you (Ephesians 1:18).

Your Body – The vessel for the Will of God

(Romans 12:1-2) KJV
"I beseech you therefore, brethren, by the mercies of God, that ye present your bodies a living sacrifice, holy, acceptable unto God, which is your reasonable service. [2] And be not conformed to this world: but be ye transformed by the renewing of your mind, that ye may prove what is that good, and acceptable, and perfect, will of God."

When we came into a covenant with God through Christ, we did so because His body was used to fulfill the greatest sacrifice that was ever made. He took the totality of the sins of the entire world upon Himself. His body endured the penalty of our sin through temptations He faced and then the condemnation that He would take. It would be the scourging of being whipped 39 times for our healing, bruised for our iniquities, forsaken by God, and dying upon the cross. His body was then placed in a tomb, and on the third day, He rose from the dead with a new resurrected body. We will have a body like His when we met Him in the sky.

This brings us to understand that we now must yield our bodies as those alive from the dead. The body of Jesus was used to die as a sacrifice that we might live. Now our bodies are a sacrifice to be used in a living way unto God. We then are called upon to "present our bodies" in a way that would be acceptable unto God and so happens to be our reasonable service.

How does this impact discovering God's Will for your life? Why can't we just expect God's Will to be known regardless of what we do with our bodies? The Will of God is alive, and it is in God who is in you. Your body remains under your violation, and God has granted you the freedom to yield to Him even as Christ yielded to Him. We have to remind ourselves that this is a relationship of wills. God is not looking to force anyone to love Him. The gospel's core is God so loved the world that He gave His only begotten Son that "Whosoever Will" believe in Him shall not perish. When we have yielded our will to His lordship, it will be made evident in what we do with our body. Do we present it to Him or to ourselves and therefore the world?

When we present our body to God as Christ did, it becomes the evidence necessary that we genuinely want to live for Him. Anything short of yielding our bodies to God is sheer religion. We can give sacrifices and offerings of all kinds, but God wants your body presented as a living sacrifice.

(Hebrews 10:5-7) KJV
"Wherefore when he cometh into the world, he saith, Sacrifice and offering thou wouldest not, but a body hast thou prepared me: [6] In burnt offerings and sacrifices for sin thou hast had no pleasure. [7] Then said I, Lo, I come (in the volume of the book it is written of me,) to do thy will, O God."

How exactly do we do that? We yield. When we are faced with a choice, be it what we wear or what we eat or where we go or what we see, God is there, and if we are yielded, we can hear Him speak to us as to whether it would be pleasing to Him. It's called conviction. When we learn to yield more to God to please Him, He sees obedience which is the only language that moves God. Obedience is the very act of drawing near to Him and the force that propels your journey. When we draw near to Him, He draws near to us because we are asking Him to.

Remember that your journey is not a hobby, something you like to do, or a job. It is the very essence of who you are. You don't arrive there once and for all; it is a perpetual place of living that transcends time and space and reaches into eternity. The streets are made of gold, and where Christ is building you a mansion in the Father's House! As you keep this frame of mind - through the renewal of your mind - with the constitution of the kingdom of God, journey living becomes first nature to you. In yielding, you are giving space to the Holy Spirit to inform you and quicken you that what you are living is true to who you are, and you can depend upon Him to sustain you and provide for your journey. You arrive at fearlessness and expectation of the manifestation of God in every area of your life.

The revelation in yielding is that you come to experience that we can do nothing without Him and that which we do is by Him and through Him. Therefore, as the mystery unfolds, we do all things in allowing Him to do them through us. Therein do we discover a peace that surpasses the need to understand and a joy that is unspeakable and full of glory.

Chapter Five

THE KINGDOM OF GOD

The simplicity of discovering and fulfilling the Will of God is found in the prayer in which Jesus taught His disciples to pray; it is The Lord's prayer. It lays in intimate and precise detail how we can and must approach God to be aligned with eternity that provides every source needed to be assured that you are indeed in His hand and fully known, protected, and cared for. Let's look at each line of this prayer of which I pray every morning and have never failed to obtain fresh revelation, power, and confidence to face the day – even when the day was sheer warfare. More importantly, however, I was allowed to come into the joyous presence of God as my loving Papa.

There are countless books and studies on the Lord's prayer. This chapter is not to be exhaustive by any means. But the primary purpose will be for looking unto discovering the Will of God for your life.

(Matthew 6:6-14) KJV

"But thou, when thou prayest, enter into thy closet, and when thou hast shut thy door, pray to thy Father which is in secret; and thy Father which seeth in secret shall reward thee openly. [7] But when ye pray, use not vain repetitions, as the heathen do: for they think that they shall be heard for their much speaking. [8] Be not ye therefore like unto them: for your Father knoweth what things ye have need of, before ye ask him. [9] After this manner therefore pray ye: Our Father which art in heaven, Hallowed be thy name. [10] Thy kingdom come. Thy will be done in earth, as it is in heaven. [11] Give us this day our daily bread. [12] And forgive us our debts, as we forgive our debtors. [13] And lead us not into temptation, but deliver us from evil: For thine is the kingdom, and the power, and the glory, for ever. Amen. [14] For if ye forgive men their trespasses, your heavenly Father will also forgive you: [15] But if ye forgive not men their trespasses, neither will your Father forgive your trespasses."

I'll be honest with you; this is so rich it will take an eternity to experience it! Before Jesus even goes into what to pray, He shows us first 'HOW' to pray. This is intimate, personal, and between only you and God. When a husband and wife as man and woman come together to become one, they do so in their own bedroom upon their own bed, and no one is there but them and the Lord. Nor is it always a sexual experience. They are sharing a space that only they share. When we come before God, it is a spiritual communion between two entities. Access to God can come only through Jesus Christ, who satisfied sins debt on our behalf. There is no other way to be welcomed into the Holy presence of God than by way of sacrifice. Jesus made that sacrifice once and for all.

Where to Pray

But thou, when thou prayest, enter into thy closet, and when thou hast shut thy door, pray to thy Father which is in secret; and thy Father which seeth in secret shall reward thee openly.

God wants our attention to be on Him alone. It is sacred, and when our eye is single, we are totally focused on the Father with nothing distracting our spirit and mind; we attract Him into our space. We get away from the noise, from the family, from people, the phone, social media, the world, and we 'close the door.' We don't announce it, share it, or promote it. It is devoted attention and affection to God your Heavenly Father. If we don't have this private space with God, our collective praying is of no or little relevance to Him. If we are more committed to prayer meetings with people and making known our needs and issues in public spaces but have not done so in the closet with the door shut, we need to question whether or not we are of the faith and born again. Religion is a powerful counterfeit and goes through all the motions of godly acts. However, it lacks the most important factor: RELATIONSHIP.

This is not a weekend adventure where we go on a retreat to get a spiritual "reboot". It is a lifestyle of daily devotion to the Heavenly Father who created you, and nothing major will happen in your mind, heart, and spirit towards the discovery of His Will until you discover that secret place every day. It becomes what you look forward to the most.

. [7] "But when ye pray, use not vain repetitions, as the heathen do: for they think that they shall be heard for their much speaking. [8] Be not ye therefore like unto them: for your Father knoweth what things ye have need of, before ye ask him."

This has to do with our attitude towards God. Religion design to avoid what God requires of us is an abomination to Him!

(Isaiah 1:12-13) KJV
"When ye come to appear before me, who hath required this at your hand, to tread my courts? [13] Bring no more vain oblations; incense is an abomination unto me; the new moons and sabbaths, the calling of assemblies, I cannot away with; it is iniquity, even the solemn meeting."

He wants us to rend our hearts and not our garments. Enough of the outward show! He does not expect perfection; He wants humility and sincerity. Jesus even clarifies that this is not even about your needs because He knows them and provides them. He is inviting us to share His heart for the Kingdom and His Will. Until we can get past our own childish objectives with God, we will always miss the invitation to experience the "high calling of God".

Now, it is time to pray in alignment with God's dispensational agenda. The coming of His Kingdom and the doing of His Will!

[9] "After this manner therefore pray ye: Our Father which art in heaven, Hallowed be thy name."

My Father

Before proceeding to issues of the Kingdom, Jesus wants us to be grounded in our newfound identity. God is now our Father! When I pray this, I am constantly realigning myself with God. As a result, whatever I missed from my earthly Father, and we all have missed something – I have found in my Heavenly Father. Our ability to proceed in the Will of God is rooted in our identity in God. It is a constant battle because Satan knows that if he can get you to question your identity with your Heavenly Father, he will persuade you to question everything else. Think about it. The only prayer that Jesus taught His disciples, and it begins with "My Father". I can't write about it enough. You need to take the time to meditate on those two words until it becomes Rhema to you and intimately connect with God because all of the Kingdom and His Will is born out of Him being "YOUR" Father!

Hallowed be thy Name

To Hallow is to Reverence. To reverence God is both by faith and by invitation. It's hard to explain because you can't reverence what or who you don't know, and you can't know until you discover, and how can you find out what you don't know because if you found it, how would you know you did? The only answer is God unveils Himself to us as we unveil ourselves to Him.

(James 4:8) KJV
"Draw nigh to God, and he will draw nigh to you. Cleanse your hands, ye sinners; and purify your hearts, ye double minded."

The evidence that we reverence Him is not that we lift our hands and sing songs but that we present our hearts to Him by seeking after Him till we find Him. This is what King David had learned in all his years and conveyed this to his son, Solomon.

(1 Chronicles 28:9) KJV
"And thou, Solomon my son, know thou the God of thy Father, and serve him with a perfect heart and with a willing mind: for the LORD searcheth all hearts, and understandeth all the imaginations of the thoughts: if thou seek him, he will be found of thee; but if thou forsake him, he will cast thee off for ever."

The discovery of God's Will for your life is the very discovery of God Himself. They are not separate, for in the entire scheme of things, God Himself is your reward. When we try to isolate God away from who we are and what we do, we fall into the subtle trap of rebellion. It is so deceptive, and it is the same deception that Lucifer fell into. Though it is speculative at best, I don't believe Lucifer was deceived in a moment; I think it took time to settle in and come to full bloom. Because God's nature is merciful, it has to reason that God gave space for Lucifer to correct himself, but he didn't. He dug in deeper.

The Kingdom of God

Likewise, Adam yielded to this same temptation when he resolved to allow his wife, Eve, to speak with the serpent and be lured into eating the forbidden fruit. He was there with her watching the entire incident and said nothing! It was actually a part of Adams's plan so that when it was time to account for what he had done, he could not blame Eve but blame God Himself for giving her to him! Think about that for a minute. We're talking about premeditated sin.

I, too, am guilty! I can think of incidents in which I reasoned why I can, why I should and why I will do this thing! It was predicated on one thing; I wanted what I wanted apart from God Himself. I had concluded that I deserved it and that somehow it was not fair that I could not have it. The back story that Lucifer, Adam, and William all have one thing in common; God was holding back on us that which was good and just.

When we reverence God, it is the purest expression that we trust Him. This trust must be reaffirmed daily and throughout the day because we will face the temptation to take matters into our own hands as long as we are in this life. Lucifer has now been cast out of heaven and is destined for an eternity of fire. He now roams about as a lion seeking whom he may devour. His method has not changed. "Hath God said" will always be his opening line because that is all he has. To question the Word of God is where he takes us time and time again. Yet, when we have resolved to Hallow God from our true heart, we willfully reject this temptation by knowingly submitting ourselves to God.

Thy Kingdom Come

We can also express it this way: Come thy Kingdom! I know you, like me, have heard the carnal accusation, " You're so heavenly-minded that you're no earthly good!" Such who would utter such a statement could only be motivated by both pride and conviction. According to the Word of God, we, who are the children of God, cannot be of any earthly good if we are not of a heavenly mindset. Heaven is the standard, not the earth. To have a significant impact upon the planet, being attuned to the kingdom is not an option or leisure. We have been granted this privilege by being predestined before the foundations of the world.

(Romans 9:11) KJV
"(For the children being not yet born, neither having done any good or evil, that the purpose of God according to election might stand, not of works, but of him that calleth;)"

Ephesians 1:11) KJV
"In whom also we have obtained an inheritance, being predestinated according to the purpose of him who worketh all things after the counsel of his own will:"

The Kingdom of God

The coming of God's Kingdom does not come with observation because it is within you. The very journey God has called you to experience is the manifestation of His Kingdom within you and then through you to the world. As you purpose to discover and fulfill God's Will, it will always be directly connected to His Kingdom – first. When we allow our minds to be renewed to this kingdom truth, we come to realize that God's Will for our lives is from and of above. This is totally contrary to the world and its systems, processes, and values. When God's people allow their natural man to dictate or interpret God's Will, it will always be measurable according to the earthly standards because the natural man cannot receive the things of God, nor can he understand them.

(1 Corinthians 2:12-14) KJV
"Now we have received, not the spirit of the world, but the spirit which is of God; that we might know the things that are freely given to us of God. [13] Which things also we speak, not in the words which man's wisdom teacheth, but which the Holy Ghost teacheth; comparing spiritual things with spiritual. [14] But the natural man receiveth not the things of the Spirit of God: for they are foolishness unto him: neither can he know them, because they are spiritually disconcerned."

The Will of God is such a mystery for most because it is not possible to know without the spirit of God teaching us to know it. God's Spirit leads us from spiritual to spiritual. However, when we refuse to align our minds and our wills with His Kingdom, we cannot discern God's Will, and therefore we

Journey By Faith

default back to what is acceptable by the world, and especially religion.

Who alone, but Jesus, made this clear?

(John 18:36) KJV
"Jesus answered, My kingdom is not of this world: if my kingdom were of this world, then would my servants fight, that I should not be delivered to the Jews: but now is my kingdom not from hence."

Let's be clear here. God's Will - will never coincide with this world's agenda, pursuits, appetites, rewards, and philosophies. When we allow ourselves to be lured into the seeking of possessions, positions, status, and the accolades of men as the desires of our hearts, we have misaligned ourselves apart from God's Kingdom. Therefore, His Will for us can never be revealed. This is so because we would never see it, believe it, or understand it. The Will of God is otherworldly and cannot be seen or understood when based on this world or the intellect. The natural man does not and never will accept the things of God. He can't!

1 Corinthians 2:14 KJV
But the natural man receiveth not the things of the Spirit of God: for they are foolishness unto him: neither can he know them, because they are spiritually discerned.

For now, Satan is the god of this world, and he boldly offered it to Jesus if He would bow down and worship him.

Let this sink in - Satan offered this world to Jesus if He bowed down and worshipped him.

Matthew 4:8-10 KJV
"Again the devil taketh him up into an exceeding high mountain, and sheweth him all the kingdoms of the world, and the glory of them; [9] And saith unto him, All these things will I give thee, if thou wilt fall down and worship me. [10] Then saith Jesus unto him, Get thee hence, Satan: for it is written, Thou shalt worship the Lord thy God, and him only shalt thou serve."

What was the thing Satan wanted from Jesus? Worship! It is also what God wants from us: Worship! The highest form of worship is obedience to God. Obedience is an act of will. It is not a song, an idea, or an abstract religious expression. It is a measurable action that reflects His Kingdom coming and His will being done through you with intent.

Thy Will Be Done

We can also say it this way; Be Done Thy Will! As we receive the kingdom within our hearts and align our spirit with it, the manifestation of His Will begins to illuminate our renewed minds. God, by His Spirit, makes us to will and to do of His good pleasure. Along with this, He imparts the faith that is suitable for the calling. Jesus is both author and the finisher of our faith. He has given you a measure of faith according to the Will of God upon your life. Even so, God gives us the faith to do His Will; we must receive it. The Word of God alone will not carry you if you don't mix it with the faith that He has given you.

(Hebrews 4:2) KJV
"For unto us was the gospel preached, as well as unto them: but the word preached did not profit them, not being mixed with faith in them that heard it."

His will being done is always in a perpetual state because it is alive. It is not stagnant or conclusive. You don't ever arrive at a place where you no longer need to strive to enter into it. When you try to make sense of it, you will no longer move in faith.

As I experience the Will of God unfolding in my life, I have come to accept more deeply the truth that this temporal life has nothing to offer me outside of His Will. I have resolved, and resolve daily, that for me to live is Christ, and to die is gain. More than anything, I want His Will done through my life. Therefore, I arrive at a place of internal peace and joy with no need to take thought for my life. Besides, if I did take thought, I wouldn't know where to start anyway! So to me, it is an awesome arrangement.

(1 Peter 4:2) KJV
"That he no longer should live the rest of his time in the flesh to the lusts of men, but to the will of God."

We arrive at a place of rest that we access by faith alone as children of God. When we extend our faith by acting on His revealed Will, God in His faithfulness confirms Himself in many ways. Some confirmations you will not notice immediately, while others you will witness right before your eyes to be miracles.

As we experience this lifestyle of faith in living in His Will, we begin to go from what's known as faith to faith and glory to glory. It simply means He keeps taking us to a higher place within Himself. We mustn't forget that HE is our exceeding and great reward – not faith itself. He is the object of our faith, not ministry, not revelation, or anything created. It is this quiet intimacy that we come to safeguard at all costs. It demands a life of humility and sacrifice to not merely maintain but abound in our faith.

The Will of God being done through your life is a treacherous assault against the devil, and therefore he will go to great lengths to circumvent your pursuit of it. He will use any means that you make available to him, whether knowingly or not. It could be family, health, finances, religion, politics, food, pleasure, materialism, gifts, associations, relationships, good intentions, good ideas, meaningful projects, and the list goes on. This is why you must discover God's Will for your life. If you don't, you will spend years doing good things, great things, hanging out with friendly people, being congratulated for outstanding accomplishments… BUT it was all for naught when weighed against the Will that God had destined you to accomplish.

What Happens Next

When you utter the words, "thy will be done," it immediately initiates heavenly activity that rules over the entire universe. It ushers in mighty angles that are assigned to you because, as well, the Will of God uttered from your spirit elevates demonic opposition against you to oppose all that God wants to accomplish through your life.

As you pray, "Thy will be done," be so conscious of those areas of your life that are before you. If you seek clarity as to what God wants of you in specific areas of your life, then pray that particular area of your life. Pray, "Lord, your will be done regarding the work that I am seeking." "Lord, your will be done as to whether or not I should enter into this relationship." Lord, your will be done as to whether or not I should get this house." You must be heart-felt and intentional as to truly wanting His Will to be done in ALL facets of your life. Your heart must be bowed before Him recognizing Him as sovereign Lord and God of your life.

When you have preserved in this prayer, His peace that surpasses all understanding will come upon you. You then will have the faith to totally trust that He has heard your petition and will work all things according to His Will. Then yield, be patient, and God will manifest His pleasure according to His time. He will reveal His mind to your mind, and in faith, you will act. When I say act, I simply mean that He will give you steps to take in keeping with His Will. You must respond in faith and take the steps. Or He will likewise give you a confirmation in your spirit to not move, and you in faith will stand. It is all found in your intimate relationship with Him rooted in a life of obedience. God will be more willing than you are to reveal to you His good pleasure.

In my own journey, when I daily pray the Lord's pray and come to this portion of His Will be done, I am specific. I talk to Him just like He is sitting next to me. He is actually closer because He is IN me. I know He hears me and loves it when I confide in Him. It never fails that as I rise and go about my day, He begins to give me instructions. I will often give those instructions back to Him because I know if they are of Him, He will give them back to me even more so. It is the relationship that we have developed over time. Once He gives them back to me, I just find myself doing it. I don't even think. I have accepted that it is His Will, and I move on it! I don't worry about the outcome because I never worried in my petition to Him. Worry is never a part of praying thy Will be done because worry is rooted in fear, and praying thy Will be done is all from a place of perfect love and trust.

"In the earth, as it is in heaven" must always be the target. When you have this as your target, you can never go wrong because it testifies that your interest is His interest and not your own. Your affections are set on things above, not on the things of this world. This is where true biblical faith and the faith of men and demons part ways. All those who teach faith for faith can never and will never incorporate it in the Lord's prayer in its entirety. They will carefully pick and choose certain elements to keep an appearance of being Christ and Kingdom-centered. Still, they fail the test miserably because there is no spirit behind their words, and they must talk, talk, and talk to keep their listeners mesmerized with feigned words to make merchandise of the blind so that they can use their money and passion for their own self agenda.

(2 Peter 2:3) KJV
"And through covetousness shall they with feigned words make merchandise of you: whose judgment now of a long time lingereth not, and their damnation slumbereth not."

Start where you are. God, in His grace, will bring you to where you need to be. Rest and remain in His peace because there is no more profound love for you than His. There is no need to be anxious for anything regardless of the reason. He controls all things - even the number of hairs on your head!

Give us this day our daily bread

This is a beautiful truth that can free you to have all the time you need to seek after God. Notice how this is at the end of the prayer? How often, when we pray for our needs, we do so at the beginning of prayer. When we accept the faithfulness of God to meet our needs, we can be attentive to Him as our Father, who is deserving of our adoration and worship first. We can attune our life to the motion and the movement of the Kingdom. Remember, Jesus even stated before we pray do not as the hypocrites or the Gentiles do for God already knows your needs.

(Matthew 6:5) KJV
"And when thou prayest, thou shalt not be as the hypocrites are: for they love to pray standing in the synagogues and in the corners of the streets, that they may be seen of men. Verily I say unto you, They have their reward."

Therefore, when it is time to pray for your daily necessities, do so in genuine faith and joy. Whatever you need, pray for them with the realization that you are in harmony with God, with His kingdom, and with the doing of His Will. You are actually worshipping Him and have a genuine expectation that He has already met your needs according to His riches in glory that is in Christ Jesus. As you are asking, you are also thanking Him for what He has already done because you know that before you call, He answers you. I emphasize that we need not pray in a spirit of fear or worry; if so, there is a disconnect in the relationship, and you need to focus on that and fix it.

For thine is the kingdom

Finally, we conclude in our prayer time as we are pursuing the discovery of His Will, with a declaration that it is all His! This causes us to have a deep assurance that we are serving the King of the universe who lives in us, and it is ALL HIS! It is HIS kingdom. HIS power. HIS glory. Forever! What could be more consuming than this? Nothing. I fear we fail to realize just WHO He is more often than we should. In fact, we can't know Who He is unless He is revealed to us by the Son. Neither can we know Who the Son is unless He is revealed to us by the Father.

(Matthew 11:27) KJV
"All things are delivered unto me of my Father: and no man knoweth the Son, but the Father; neither knoweth any man the Father, save the Son, and he to whomsoever the Son will reveal him."

The only thing that keeps us from receiving this revelation is our unwillingness to surrender to Him, our heart of hearts. We have a reservation about falling down before Him daily in adoration and praise. We somehow don't fully accept that apart from Him, we can do nothing. Therefore, we search out systems and yield to the schemes of men to accomplish the Will of heaven [QR CODE].

The tragic truth is that more souls than we can imagine will be deceived because they don't want the truth. Deep within the wretchedness of our hearts, we, like Judas, betray Jesus, and to do so with a kiss! Judas walked with Jesus for three years, heard His Word, witnessed His miracles, and yet, he would not submit his heart of hearts to Jesus. He, therefore, became a perfect victim for the devil who would use the wisdom and rationale of the natural man that caused Judas to justify himself in turning against the Son of God. Jesus said it would have been better for him not to have been born! There is a Judas in all of us because we are the seed of Adam. Our nature seeks ways to rule even above the rule of God's Kingdom and the doing of His Will.

I close this chapter with this hope: That each of us would fully embrace the surpassing wonders and perfect love that God has for each of us. To reject the lie of the enemy of our souls, that God is unjust in wanting and deserving of our adoration, of our souls, and the submitting of ourselves to His Will. He is good because no one else is. He has prepared incredible blessings for us that will be ours throughout eternity - world without end! May we not miss it!

Chapter Six

Going on to Perfection

If we were to take account of our own spiritual growth, where would we place ourselves? How would we judge ourselves, and what would we discover? Would we be found reprobates? Would we have confidence in the face of Jesus Christ Himself that we are where we should be? Can we simply face the mirror and have peace that we are walking where we have attained, or are we convicted as we reflect on our lack of spiritual fervor and attentiveness?

These are serious questions. Questions that extend past this temporal life and have consequences that reach throughout eternity. We have been commanded to examine ourselves to ascertain as to whether we are even saved! I am persuaded beyond a doubt that countless souls have confessed Christ with their mouths but have never received Him in their hearts. Actually, I need no persuasion because the Word of God declared that such would depart from the faith. *(Romans 10:10) KJV*

For with the heart man believeth unto righteousness; and with the mouth confession is made unto salvation.

(1 Timothy 4:1) KJV
"Now the Spirit speaketh expressly, that in the latter times some shall depart from the faith, giving heed to seducing spirits, and doctrines of devils;"

As we take up the heavenly invitation to "go on to perfection", let us begin examining ourselves within our own closet of humble prayer. Let us come before the loving Father, knowing that He welcomes us without wrath into His bosom to discover who we are and where we are with Him. Then, when we present ourselves in lowliness of heart, He will hear us and help us.

(2 Corinthians 13:5) KJV
"Examine yourselves, whether ye be in the faith; prove your own selves. Know ye not your own selves, how that Jesus Christ is in you, except ye be reprobates?"

(2 Corinthians 13:5) AMP
"Test and evaluate yourselves to see whether you are in the faith and living your lives as [committed] believers. Examine yourselves [not me]! Or do you not recognize this about yourselves [by an ongoing experience] that Jesus Christ is in you—unless indeed you fail the test and are rejected as counterfeit?"

Going on to Perfection

There is an eternal danger of not discovering God's Will should we resist this admonishment to examine ourselves. God will not be mocked because what we sow is that which we shall reap (Galatians 6:7). The longsuffering of God cannot be fathomed. However, God does have His limits.

For years, I struggled in a specific area of my life that kept me from moving to a higher place of effectiveness for the Lord. I was not effective because I was not perfecting my relationship with Him. I came to realize that what I desired more than anything was a perfect heart towards God and a joyous peace when my eyes opened in the morning time. God, in His mercy, knew I didn't have the answers or the ability to deal with this in my own strength. However, I knew that God could not have the desire for me to want to be free. That desire had to be my own. I begin to realize that the excuses were wearing thin, and all that I knew about God was eroding my justifications for tolerating this issue in my life. It would be that reality that drove me to my knees in fear of having to be judged by God that caused me to cry out from the depths of my soul. I cuddle up on my bed like a baby crying out to God. I then moved to the floor and prostrated myself before Him and asked Him for help. It would not come in that very second, but it came within days as I remained in that place of deep sorrow and repentance.

I tore the T-Shirt that I was wearing in sheer desperation to break free from that place of rebellion and compromise. I keep that T-shirt hanging where I can see it every day and touch it to keep me in remembrance that I'm not going back! I can't go back! I want to go on to perfection! I love my Heavenly Father and want to please Him. I fully accepted that when Christ died – I indeed died, and when He rose from the dead, I indeed rose from the dead with Him. I, therefore, will no longer live to dead things! I had my deliverance and have kept it and will keep it forever because Christ died once for sin, and therefore so did I!

When God speaks of perfection, He's not talking about how good you are at what you do. How good you are as a person, has nothing to do with the effectiveness of His Will working through you. Instead, it is how perfectly you are walking with God that establishes you with Him and causes everything to work together for your good. So it is that you <u>LOVE</u> God, and you want to pursue the <u>CALL</u> He has for you according to His PURPOSE.

(Romans 8:28) KJV
"And we know that all things work together for good to them that love God, to them who are the called according to his purpose."

We deceive ourselves when we want to identify with our gift and talent and not where we are with God – one on one.

We create a false spiritual place when we are deceived into placing value on ourselves because of what we do.

I am part of a beautiful church family.

- I go to church every Sunday.
- I give my 10% plus a few extra dollars.
- I'm a decent person.
- I coach the baseball team.
- I mentor a few people.
- I serve on the deacon board.
- I pet every dog I see.
- I'm super kind to people.
- I'm not prejudiced.
- I'm not this.
- I'm not that.
- I'm, I'm, I'm!

If you think you can define what is righteous before a Holy God, who is a consuming fire, you will spend the rest of your life justifying yourself until you die. You will then stand before the judgment seat of Christ and repeat all this to Him and come to find out in a thundering truth that you refused over and over to accept...

(Isaiah 64:6) KJV
"But we are all as an unclean thing, and all our righteousnesses are as filthy rags; and we all do fade as a leaf; and our iniquities, like the wind, have taken us away."

We might very well do these things, but should we use them to shelter our hearts from being presented to God and going on to a more perfect place with Him, we make them idols. When there is an idol in one's life, it is made evident in your LIFESTYLE!

My grandmother used to say, "Gerald (my middle name), baby, when you boil it down, the truth will come out!" So, when we take all our reasons and explanations, and put them in a pot and boil them, what will be left is how we live! LIFESTYLE. What exactly am I saying? Jesus made it so plain.

(Matthew 12:33) KJV
"Either make the tree good, and his fruit good; or else make the tree corrupt, and his fruit corrupt: for the tree is known by his faith."

The fruit here is not deeds of works that we choose, but fruit that can only be borne of the Spirit. If it is so, it must come through right standing with God alone. 'Right standing' is of the heart, not of works. It is the fruit of the Spirit that first testifies of who we are.

(Galatians 5:22-26) KJV

"But the fruit of the Spirit is love, joy, peace, longsuffering, gentleness, goodness, faith, [23] Meekness, temperance: against such there is no law. [24] And they that are Christ's have crucified the flesh with the affections and lusts. [25] If we live in the Spirit, let us also walk in the Spirit. [26] Let us not be desirous of vain glory, provoking one another, envying one another."

The discovery of the will of God is a result of the discovery of God Himself within you. The Kingdom of God does not come with observation. It is not a matter of what you do, by way of works. It is a result of Christ working in you for you, and therefore the first fruits will be that of the Spirit followed by our works that come forth from the Spirit.

Therefore, when we judge ourselves, we do so with the fruit of the Spirit being our standard, not the works of deeds or of the flesh.

- Am I walking in the Love of God?
- Is there a joy I have within myself that is not based on the external?
- Do I possess a peace that is evident to others?
- Am I longsuffering in the midst of pressing circumstances?
- Am I gentle with my own emotions and towards others I know and don't know?

- Meekness, temperance are both attributes that reflect the ability to manage emotions regardless of the circumstances you might be faced with.
- Is your flesh in control of you? Do you eat what you want, when you want, and how much you want without regard to the Spirit's direction?
- Do you fast and pray as a matter of practice? Fasting and prayer are not an option. Jesus said, "WHEN" you fast and pray, not "IF."
- Are you given to fleshly habits that you cannot control?
- If single, are you sexually active which is fornication?
- Are your affections under the rule of the Spirit, or can they spiral out of control given the right atmosphere?
- Are you envious of others and are tempted to outdo someone, some church, or some ministry?
- Are you in pursuit of the glory of men? This is primarily a temptation amongst those in leadership. Always seeking to know people who are known to consider yourself as someone who has attained status.
- Your agenda is based on what you say and do and not solely being pleasing to the Heavenly Father, aside from works.
- You compete and remove any possible threat that causes you to feel intimidated. The simple act of returning a phone call is beyond you because they don't "rank" or offer you any possible opportunity to advance yourself.

If we have succumbed to this fruit, we are lighter than vanity and have deceived ourselves into a false place of relationship with Jesus. In fact, if and when we persist in such a spirit, we can and will be given over to a reprobate mind. We then exchange the truth for a lie and follow a different Jesus and Gospel without even knowing it.

(Galatians 1:6-7) KJV
"I marvel that ye are so soon removed from him that called you into the grace of Christ unto another gospel: [7] Which is not another; but there be some that trouble you, and would pervert the gospel of Christ."

Self-examination is paramount to spiritual maturity. It is a characteristic that accompanies those striving to "go on to perfection" in the spiritual life with God. It attracts God's attention, and He will give you the grace to recognize areas of your life that must be brought under His Lordship if you are to make the next transition in your life in spiritual development.

What Is Perfection?

(Philippians 3:15-16) KJV
"Let us therefore, as many as be perfect, be thus minded: and if in any thing ye be otherwise minded, God shall reveal even this unto you. [16] Nevertheless, whereto we have already attained, let us walk by the same rule, let us mind the same thing."

Perfect in the simplest terms is "walking where you have already attained". Doing what you know is what God requires of you. Living at the standard of righteousness according to the truth that has been revealed is what pleases Him.

- Do you know to forgive those who have wronged you?
  - Have you forgiven them?
- Do you know to give bountifully?
  - Do you instead give sparingly?
- Do you know to love your wife as Christ loves the church?
  - Are you rather impatient and bossy?
- Do you know to submit yourself to your husband as unto the Lord and be a helpmeet to him?
  - Are you nagging him or comparing him with another man in your mind?

Again, our "lifestyle" testifies to where we are spiritually. If we live in a place of maturity, we will demonstrate a stable faith that propels us daily in the journey that God has us experiencing. We will also be natural encouragers of the faith of others by sheer demonstration of our life even if we said nothing or very little. Our life is an epistle read of men.

Either discovering His Will or carrying out His Will, you have moved beyond the elementary foundation of God's Word when you are walking in and towards perfection. Instead, you are learning to discern both good and evil. You have also come to a place where you will not tolerate certain behaviors.

(Hebrews 6:1-6) KJV
"Therefore leaving the principles of the doctrine of Christ, let us go on unto perfection; not laying again the foundation of repentance from dead works, and of faith toward God, [2] Of the doctrine of baptisms, and of laying on of hands, and of resurrection of the dead, and of eternal judgment. [3] And this will we do, if God permit. [4] For it is impossible for those who were once enlightened, and have tasted of the heavenly gift, and were made partakers of the Holy Ghost, [5] And have tasted the good word of God, and the powers of the world to come, [6] If they shall fall away, to renew them again unto repentance; seeing they crucify to themselves the Son of God afresh, and put him to an open shame."

This block of scripture can be the basis of an entire book! So, I want to hit this quickly and point out some very critical and obvious truth.

1. V. 1 The first mark of perfection is that you don't tolerate deadness in your life. You don't play with sin or those who do. You have accepted and continued to receive the completed work of Christ on the cross for your sanctification and obedience. You apply grace to obey, not to justify an immature lifestyle, and, therefore, always in need of repenting of the same thing.

2. V. 1-3 Just think of the time that so many Christians waste in discussing the doctrine of baptism, speaking in new tongues, laying on of hands, the resurrection,

and eternal judgment. Yet, they never go beyond that. They look for more knowledge just to argue better. If any, they have minimal experience in doing the Will of God – if they even know it. Such truths we entrust to God as we go on to do His Will.

3. V. 4-6 The full impact of the impossibility of being renewed to repentance is when we insist on our sins. Even as Judas betrayed Jesus with a kiss – many such are doing so today. Let the scripture speak clearly that once God has rejected you for falling away, you will not be renewed to repentance because you will not seek after it. In fact, God gives you over to a reprobate mind altogether, and you begin to see good as evil and evil as good (Romans 1:28). The scripture tells us not to argue with such a person because they are self-condemned and taken captive by the devil to do his will (Titus 3:10, 11; 2 Timothy 2:26). Such conscience has been seared with a hot iron (1 Timothy 4:2), and they think they are right when they are on a highway to HELL!

Your Walk Matters

It grieves God when His people quote scriptures, boasts of degrees in theology, demands they be addressed with status titles, and regularly prophesy what He is about to do, yet their walk reveals more than their words ever could. Since the beginning of time, with Adam being the first perpetrator, men have always tried to separate their actions from their talk. Adam boldly took the fruit from his wife's hand and ate it. He did this after he watches her eat it first after discussing it with the serpent. Adam did not once object! When it was time to give an account to God, he blamed God to His face for giving him the woman! The pattern is always the same. Regardless of how hard we try to avoid it through a play on the grace of God to justify not obeying Him, grace will never be the justification for disobedience and sin because grace more abounds than sin, that we sin not!

(Romans 6:1-2) KJV
"What shall we say then? Shall we continue in sin, that grace may abound? [2] God forbid. How shall we, that are dead to sin, live any longer then?"

The only way to abound with God is to please God, and the way you please God is by your walk, not your knowledge.

(1 Thessalonians 4:1) KJV
"Furthermore then we beseech you, brethren, and exhort you by the Lord Jesus, that as ye have received of us how ye ought to walk and to please God, so ye would abound more and more."

Pleasing God is perfection. Not please God is not perfection. Believe it or not, some believe they can please God without doing a thing. They neutralize the need to bring forth fruit by totally abolishing God's demands for evidence of His working in our lives. I'll let Jesus' own Words settle that:

(Matthew 12:33) KJV
"Either make the tree good, and his fruit good; or else make the tree corrupt, and his fruit corrupt: for the tree is known by his fruit."

Keeping your body under

(1 Corinthians 9:27) KJV
[27] "But I keep under my body, and bring it into subjection: lest that by any means, when I have preached to others, I myself should be acastaway."

Perfection is not an idea, an imagination, or a 'state of being.' Perfection is a tangible expression of how you are literally (not figuratively) living your spiritual life as manifested through your body. Jesus did not die metaphysically. He did literally on a cross and for three days was in a tomb. Jesus then rose from the dead with the evidence of nail scars in His hands and a stab womb in His side. He has also received the keys of death and hell as evidence of His authority overall power. Therefore, through His life, we have been raised from death and sin. Our bodies are His by legal right in which His Spirit dwells.

Paul made it plain by declaring that "I" keep my body under and bring it into subjection. This is a willful act of submission, not by works of our own efforts, but by submitting to the resurrection of Christ.

Perfection will be elusive and a far-fetched impossibility if you refuse to render your body dead to sin. This is not about 'not' sinning. It is about an attitude of working out your salvation in fear and trembling and relying on the power of the cross to walk in the Spirit so that you would not fulfill the lust of the flesh. The difference between a lamb and a pig is that though the lamb gets stuck in the mud sometimes, they are not comfortable in it and try to get out. Whereas the pig is right at home and is looking for ways to stay in it.

You and I must exercise restraint should we transition to perfection by keeping our bodies under. We do this by exercising ourselves in godliness and practice saying "no" to lifestyle choices that compromise our spiritual life. An example of this is that we should refuse to watch specific programming that tangibly grieves the Lord. In other words, if you can literally feel that the Lord disapproves, you will feel the conviction of it immediately. At that moment, you must confront what your eye wants to see and submit it with the authority of the scriptures. It's not about persuading your body with self-willed efforts. That will never work. It is about declaring the scriptures as it pertains to that issue and brings your body under the authority of that Word.

If tempted to put wickedness before your eyes:

(Psalm 101:3) KJV
"I will set no wicked thing before mine eyes: I hate the work of them that turn aside; it shall not cleave tome."

If tempted to lust:

(Matthew 5:28) KJV
[28] "But I say unto you, That whosoever looketh on a woman to lust after her hath committed adultery with her already in his heart."

What's my point? God has provided all that we need to walk perfectly before Him. In fact, in every temptation, the Lord is faithful and will provide a way of an escape that we may bear it.

(1 Corinthians 10:13) KJV
[13] "There hath no temptation taken you but such as is common to man: but God is faithful, who will not suffer you to be tempted above that ye are able; but will with the temptation also make a way to escape, that ye may be able to bear it."

Then why do we fail, you might ask? Because we want what we want. That's as simple as it gets. When we allow the flesh to rule us, we yield to it. However, if we want our Spirit to lead us, we must yield to it, and the quickening power of His resurrection will enable us to be free from the flesh in that very instant of decision.

Keeping your body under is far easier than allowing it to become emboldened, making it more difficult for you to manage. Remembering this fundamental principle will make your walk more spiritual and therefore more effective in discovering God's will daily and fulfilling it.

Distractions

(Hebrews 12:1) KJV
"Wherefore seeing we also are compassed about with so great a cloud of witnesses, let us lay aside every weight, and the sin which doth so easily beset us, and let us run with patience the race that is set before us,"

This is speaking directly to your will. Not to your Spirit, or to your imagination, but to your volition. In fact, it follows the chapter of faith, and we are placed on notice that we are being watched by a great cloud of witnesses. Who are these witnesses? We can deduce that they are those who proceeded before us, as described in Chapter 11. I don't think it would be a stretch to imagine that it could be our loved ones watching us as well.

The solution is presented to us without the need of an exegesis, extravagant preaching, or a profound teacher. It tells us to straight out "lay aside." When the eternal weight of God's Word tells you that you can lay it aside, then you can. The commands of God also carry with it the enabling of God! This is why Jesus had to only say to Satan when tempted after His 40 days of fasting, "Get thee behind me, for IT IS WRITTEN."

Take notice that we are first admonished to lay aside "every weight". There are things in our life that are not sins, but they are weights. These can be a variety of habits and choices that do not serve us in serving the Lord. I often hear the Lord say to me throughout the day if I am doing something or watch something which is not a sin. He'll say, " Not relevant, William." I've become used to it, and though not as quick as I want to be, I've gotten a lot quicker than I used to be to lay it aside. I'm down to seconds, whereas it was minutes, hours, and days. I permitted these things at a time in my life but realized if I'm to go on to perfection, they must go because they simply are not worth it. Futhermore, the devil will use the smallest of distractions to circumvent you throughout the day. He knows if he can't get you to quit, the next best thing is to slow you down and keep you from getting His will done altogether. He will cut in on your race if you let him!

Galatians 5:7-9 KJV
Ye did run well; who did hinder you that ye should not obey the truth? [8] This persuasion cometh not of him that calleth you. [9] A little leaven leaveneth the whole lump.

When you desire to please God, His grace will be more than enough for you to become that living sacrifice that He desires you to be. Sacrifices can only be made willingly with the condition that you don't have to. Otherwise, how would God know we love Him?

What about the sin that so easily beset you? By the fact of His resurrection declared, you can set it aside! It is not according to persuasion, self-power, or any other concoction of carnal effort to stop sinning. In the declaration, "I through Christ am dead to sin," and therefore, I lay it aside in Jesus Name!" When you make this declaration, remain in the frame of spiritual warfare, and as you confront this weight or sin, its power over you will weaken also in the natural until you are free. You will have to engage in multiple battles to get your final victory, but you will.

A good conscience towards God

(1 Peter 3:21) KJV
[21] "The like figure whereunto even baptism doth also now save us (not the putting away of the filth of the flesh, but the answer of a good conscience toward God,) by the resurrection of Jesus Christ:"

When I stand before God in prayer, there is nothing more powerful than a good conscience! It gives me a boldness to enter His presence, knowing that I please Him. What better position can we place ourselves in if we want to discover His

Will and then do it? If we allow our conscience to regulate our activity, we will know what God wants of us and what does not please Him.

An example of that is right this moment as I write this book. I've been distracted by other various activities that are going on online and on my phone. The Lord said, "William...." He didn't have to tell me why He called my name. Two thoughts immediately followed. Close your browser and cut off your phone. I did. Those two things though not sin proved to be a weight that distracted me from writing, and I laid it aside so that I might be able to answer with a good conscience toward God.

In your quest for the knowledge of God's will to be revealed and then the faith to fulfill His will daily, obedience will be the gateway to the reality of His manifested will unfolding moment by moment.

Going on to Perfection

Chapter Seven

Rewards and Loss

The time of this life is but a vapor, and the trouble we endure pales to nothingness which can never be compared with the glory that will be revealed in us at His appearing. We will enjoy explicit and eternal joy in the presence of God within the eternal reign of His Kingdom. Even before the eternal reign within new heaven and a new earth, we will, as the Body of Christ, rule on this earth for a millennium – which is 1,000 years! He will rule over Jerusalem, sitting on the throne of King David fulfilling prophecy. The details of this millennial reign are filled with such privilege; why wouldn't we give our absolute all to God to ensure that we miss nothing of what He has planned for us on the backdrop of eternity.

This Journey is Eternal

However, be warned! Heaven will not be equal. It is not a one fits all eternity. It will be as personal and intimate to each of us as we have allowed God to be to us in this life.

There will be levels of heaven, both horizontal and vertical, that will not be the same. Our rewards will reflect the life of faith lived, service rendered, sacrifices made, and even those who gave the ultimate – death.

While we enjoy the presence of God and of Jesus in heaven, we are doing so within the sphere that we know Him as well as allowing Him to know us. When you think about it, it only make sense.

(1 Corinthians 3:11-15) KJV
[11] "For other foundation can no man lay than that is laid, which is Jesus Christ. [12] Now if any man build upon this foundation gold, silver, precious stones, wood, hay, stubble; [13] Every man's work shall be made manifest: for the day shall declare it, because it shall be revealed by fire; and the fire shall try every man's work of what sort it is. [14] If any man's work abide which he hath built thereupon, he shall receive a reward. [15] If any man's work shall be burned, he shall suffer loss: but he himself shall be saved; yet so as by fire."

In this dispensation of grace, we are in a building phase. We must be aware that we are building upon the right foundation, and that foundation is Jesus Christ. It is not a denomination, an education, works, or any form of creation. It is Jesus Christ Himself grounded in a real relationship. A relationship in which Jesus knows you and you know Him – intimately.

Rewards and Losses

(Matthew 7:22-23) KJV
"Many will say to me in that day, Lord, Lord, have we not prophesied in thy name? and in thy name have cast out devils? and in thy name done many wonderful works? [23] And then will I profess unto them, I never knew you: depart from me, ye that work iniquity."

The tragedy that "many" will face on that day is that they will hear the most dreaded and horrific words they have ever heard. *"I NEVER knew you: depart from me, ye that work iniquity.* They approached Him with the works they did, not with a relationship they had. They built those works on another foundation other than Christ, and therefore their works accounted for nothing. While our works do not save us, they prove that we have been saved and have a relationship with God rooted in obedience to His Will. If a person does know the Lord and their works are burned, they are yet welcomed into heaven. Their welcome is not one to be proud of because they made it by fire and have suffered an immeasurable loss. While we can't imagine the dual emotion of both awe that we are standing in the presence of God at the judgment seat of Christ and the dread of loss, they are real. As we will be elated at the hope of great reward, we will equally feel the sting, shame, and remorse if we suffer loss.

(1 John 2:28) KJV
"And now, little children, abide in him; that, when he shall appear, we may have confidence, and not be ashamed before him at his coming."

Journey By Faith

Ashamed before Him at His coming?! Is that even possible? Yet, that's precisely what the Word is telling us. Just imagine that your parents have been gone on a trip for a month and you have missed them deeply. You just can't wait to be in their presence again. Though you know they are due back any day, you've lost track of exactly when. You've been lax and had decided you'd clean up the house in time before they arrive. To your horror, you hear the garage door opening on Sunday right before noon as you are watching the playoff in the living room. Your gut just got punched, and a cold sweat just hit your forehead. You think for a second and realize that no one else has a garage door opening, so it has to be them. There is nothing you can do. It is simply too late.

You're happy that they are home but ashamed that you were not ready to greet them. Instead, they walk in greeted with the leftovers in the kitchen, piled up laundry, and what appears to be a last-minute get-together in the living room with friends. Do you get the feeling? What do you do? They are still mom and dad. You hug them, and they embrace you with a sense of disappointment. Yet now there is the reckoning coming, and you will suffer loss because you knew what was required of you, and you didn't do it.

The reality of His Will for your life has the consequence of both rewards and loss. Should this not cause you to have a reverence and a fear for God and His Kingdom, then you will never give Him the honor due Him because you will have no godly fear that motivates you to be right with Him. Instead, there will be a carelessness that clouds your perspective and alters your judgment based on emotion and non-scriptural ideas.

It will be this delusion that causes you to build upon Christ with anything (wood, hay, stubble). The danger of this is that making it by fire conveys that you barely make it in. That means that you could have forfeited your very salvation! Of course, there will be those who believe that you are always saved regardless of how you live. They will argue we are not saved by works, nor can we lose our salvation no matter what we do. Of course. I mean, why would they agree. If you can eat at the tables of demons and still go to heaven – keep eating! If you can serve God and mammon and still go to heaven, keep serving man. For that matter, why even confess Christ if the unbeliever can do what they do and go to heaven merely because they said, Lord, Lord. For that matter, how would God even judge the world! Why then would God permit divorce between a husband and wife in the natural for the reason of adultery? Because if we commit spiritual adultery against Him – that's right, He will divorce us. He will not be mocked!

(Romans 3:5-7) KJV
"But if our unrighteousness commend the righteousness of God, what shall we say? Is God unrighteous who taketh vengeance? (I speak as a man) [6] God forbid: for then how shall God judge the world? [7] For if the truth of God hath more abounded through my lie unto his glory; why yet am I also judged as a sinner?"

Jesus never once suggested that we labor in vain. On the contrary, the demands He ever made were followed with promises of rewards that superseded any sacrifice rendered on behalf of Him and His Kingdom.

(Mark 10:29-30) KJV
"And Jesus answered and said, Verily I say unto you, There is no man that hath left house, or brethren, or sisters, or father, or mother, or wife, or children, or lands, for my sake, and the gospel's, [30] But he shall receive an hundredfold now in this time, houses, and brethren, and sisters, and mothers, and children, and lands, with persecutions; and in the world to come eternal life."

We are told that "every man's work shall be made manifest: for the day shall declare, because it shall be revealed by fire; and the fire shall try every man's work of what sort it is."

This should provoke us to serious attention and to what we are doing with our lives for Christ. The only way to be ignorant is to refuse to spend time in the Word of God. And there are many Christians who don't know what they believe and what God requires of them. They believe whatever the pastor teaches them is enough, and when the day is far spent and the last breath is breathed, standing before the fire that shall try each of our works will be the ultimate of all tests. There is no excuse for this. If a person will take the time to be sure that the salesman of their new Mercedes is telling the truth by reading the contract before they sign it, why don't they be sure the preacher is telling the truth by reading the spiritual covenant for themselves? THE BIBLE! People are ignorant because they choose to be.

This fire will have no agenda but to burn that which can be burned. It will consume that which can be destroyed, and that which will remain shall prove to be true. That which is burned never was. This fire will be no respecter of persons, and the manifestation of each of our labors shall be made manifest, and the day will declare it. Which signifies this will not be kept a secret. Everyone will know what your reward is as well as what your loss is.

Back to the parents coming home on Sunday unannounced. What if the parents decided to do a Facebook live after the initial shock of their son's failure to be responsible? They exposed what he had done and determined the consequences before everyone. What kind of comments do you think people would leave?

The beautiful side of this is that when the fire tries our labors, and they prove to be gold, silver, and precious stones, everyone will see this and be awed at the life we lived for Christ. This is the highest form of exaltation that matters because it is for eternity. So, as you are striving to comprehend your purpose and move forward on the journey that God has reserved for you, know that the rewards are a central theme of God's kingdom, and your faith will be rewarded throughout eternity!

Let us be ever mindful that God is a rewarder!

(Hebrews 11:6) KJV
[6] "But without faith it is impossible to please him : for he that cometh to God must believe that he is, and that he is a rewarder of them that diligently seek him."

I had a very down-to-earth conversation with God just minutes before this writing session. I shared an issue of my heart with Him that I have never done before. It had to do with rewards. As for my own walk with God, it has never been accompanied by supernatural evidence. I have not seen the Lord or heard audible His voice. Though I have had some confirming moments, they have not been likened to Isaiah or Daniel by any stretch of the imagination. I have believed though I have not seen. My question to Him was not of doubt but to me of reality. I was humbled and yet very upfront. So, I asked Him, "God, what if my life concludes and none of what I believed was true?" His answer was directly from the Bible.

"William, there is more of a blessing for you than for those who see. Remember I said that it is more blessed to believe and have not seen." I accepted that and was grateful that such scripture that I had read for many years became Rhema to me like I had never heard it. It reinforced that "faith" is the evidence of things not seen. I also realize that I could not write this book had I not yielded to the journey of faith in my own life! It would not indeed be a journey "of faith," now, would it?

Even though I wanted a certain kind of evidence, God granted me what I needed, and I humbly received it. So I have these moments, and there is a peace and a realness when I know I can approach Him – not with doubt – but with a genuine heart about anything, and He will not reject me but love me.

There are many issues in our hearts that are deep. Unless we are willing to go there and talk with God about them, we will make dangerous assumptions about God that are not true. Though we have read the Bible countless times, without an open heart, we remain guarded even against the Word staring us in the face and therefore create a false narrative regarding how God wants to reward us for our labors.

It is like God to reward His children! He will not only reward us in the life to come but in this life! Oh, how He has

Journey By Faith

blessed me! As you reflect on your journey up to this day, you can also see the kindness of God and how He has favored you.

As you purpose in your heart at this stage in your life to grab hold of God's revealed Will for you and take up your journey by faith, let it be settled that His reward is with Him. He will not be in debt to anything or anyone. Jesus has given us His Word that He has gone to prepare a place for us, to build mansions for us in the Father's House. The material He is using is the very labors that pour out of us in sacrificial living and the fulfilling of His Will. It is the gold, the silver, and the precious stones. Let us take no thought for our lives because He has it securely in His mighty hands.

Rewards and Losses

Chapter Eight

Dead Faith

James, an Apostle of Jesus Christ, declares what faith is and what it isn't. He then proposes a question to those who claim to have faith while putting their faith to the test.

James 2:17-20 KJV
Even so faith, if it hath not works, is dead, being alone. [18] Yea, a man may say, Thou hast faith, and I have works: shew me thy faith without thy works, and I will shew thee my faith by my works. [19] Thou believest that there is one God; thou doest well: the devils also believe, and tremble. [20] But wilt thou know, O vain man, that faith without works is dead?

James 2:20 AMP
But are you willing to recognize, you foolish [spiritually shallow] person, that faith without [good] works is useless?

This definition of faith, followed by the question, is not to unbelievers. It is to those who claim faith, but in actuality, some have no works. They are spiritually shallow and dormant. Isn't this the case amongst many professing Christians today? In fact, I boldly attest that most churches are nothing more than stations of confession! They gather to merely sing a few songs and to gloat in how great God is and how wonderful Jesus has been in saving them from hell, while they continue to ask God to heal their toe and save Uncle Joe for the 15th time! However, should the average professing Christian be required to detail their faith by evidence of works, many would flounder and resort to a religious canned answer that evades the question.

This is simply the truth of the condition of the majority of Churches in America. It is the very reason why our nation is imploding! What testifies of a vibrant Church is the condition of that nation. I will qualify this statement by declaring that if God has moved towards the soon return of His Son, it would be the exception. Nothing will stop God's prophetic timeline for the return of Christ and, therefore, the falling away of many who profess Him.

The Church is the salt of the earth. She is commissioned to fulfill her mandate through a journey by faith. God has called each of us in the Body of Christ to accomplish a specific Will that comes from Him. If this truth convicts your conscience, allow it to work repentance in your heart so that you would repent and submit yourself under the mighty hand of God!

Dead Faith

Only through repentance can we return and be reestablish in right standing with Abba. So let›s take a closer look at what James is defining as genuine faith.

Faith, if it hath not works, is dead being alone

All activity of church life, religious observations, and even the indulgence of more biblical knowledge equates to spiritual death if you refuse the reality of your journey. Effort, time, money, energy, and the works of men combined, cannot replace the **WORK** that testifies of **YOUR** faith. The **WORK** is the journey God has called you to tangibly live. It is the only evidence of your faith recognized by the spiritual realm that you have biblical faith that is honored by God and even acknowledged by your adversary, the devil!

What is apparent by this one verse is that a person can have faith – but it is a dead faith! Imagine having a hand, but your hand is dead. An eye, but it is blind. An ear, but it is deaf. A banking account, but it is empty. Another example is that you can have one of the best-built automobiles that money can buy, but it will die if you don›t drive it! It will fall apart, and that is especially true of a diesel engine.

What has happened to us as Christians? What has caused us to settle for nothing more than worshipping the program, the system, and the pursuit of the accolades of filthy and vain man! We have been mesmerized to the point that I fear, will take a severe shaking and chastisement for God to get our attention for us to realize most of our faith is DEAD! We are not producing the fruit of righteousness and bringing souls into the Kingdom of God that should be to the level of our supposed knowledge and resources. This is why each of us – let me repeat it – EACH of us must work out our own salvation in fear and trembling. This means you›d better know God for yourself and be able to hear His voice and DO what HE has told YOU to DO! If you are waiting for a man to give you permission to obey GOD and to approve your work, then I›m telling you now, you need to check whether you are even in a legitimate relationship with God!

Hebrews 8:11 KJV
And they shall not teach every man his neighbour, and every man his brother, saying, Know the Lord: for all shall know me, from the least to the greatest.

I will shew thee my faith by my works.

Faith is nothing to talk about. It is demonstrated by what one does. It is the actual language of heaven. God only recognized what we do with what He reveals to us. He isn›t impressed by how great we sound when we sing, how powerful we are when we preach, and many spins we can do when we dance and what awe we cause when we articulate the word of God! After all of this, God has His hand on His chin, waiting for you to

Dead Faith

do the WORK! That›s when He sits up and pays attention. That›s when the angles perk up and are prepared to carry out what God is about to do through you. That›s when the devil gets defensive because you have placed yourself in an offensive posture, and the gates of HELL will not prevail against you!

We SHOW our faith, not boast our faith. The journey by faith is actually a journey «of works» by faith. Your journey is your testimony of faith! It is the Olympics of faith. Can you imagine a sport that involved athletes talking about what they can do? Two boxers in the ring with gloves on, standing face to face talking each other down about what they can do to each other. They never break a sweat, throw a punch, get a bruise, get knocked down, or use their training to actually FIGHT! They are just «jaw-jacking.» Now, look at the crowd. They get excited about what the boxers say to each other and even shout «glory» once in a while. Some are stupid enough to throw money at the boxers for what they said, which was supposedly «deep.» Do you get the picture? This is what most churches look like today. No one is throwing punches; they are just «jaw-jacking.»

James says this: I will show you my faith by my works. I will show you that I am a faithful boxer by knocking down my enemy. I will show you I have faith by swinging, jabbing, ducking, and dancing in the ring to face down my opponent as I take my journey. I will obey God's voice and do His Will, and my works will show you that I have faith to do so.

The devils also believe

Evangelizing in America has allowed me to share with many people from different backgrounds and levels of faith. I have concluded that many people have confused belief with faith. I would venture to say that Satan has deceived millions into believing they have a relevant relationship with God because they simply believe. They have persuaded themselves that they are Christians based on the mental fact that they believe God exists. Other baseless phrases and religious pitfalls have placed souls in bondage to a dangerous trap that is ultimately rooted in self-righteousness. This lying Spirit tells them things as, you're okay, God understands you, God got you, God is your friend, God is good all the time and all the time God is good, Hang in there and just believe, He understands your heart. Thousands of words and ideas have, if not altogether, deceived people into false salvation; it has for certain minimized well-meaning Christians from using their faith to discover and fulfill God's will. Therefore, if they do make it into heaven, it will be as by fire with very little rewards.

I realize you may want to disqualify all that I'm saying because you think I am critical. Very well. To be honest, I don't think I'm critical enough. You also need to judge righteous judgment. It is not about me! I›m just a messenger to speak the truth God has given me to speak and to do so with the Spirit of fervency and urgency! The hour is late, and there are eternal dividends at stake. The Gospel was never intended to be received by the masses. Nor was it to be as easy as uttering a phrase out of your mouth. It is full of offense. In fact, Jesus offended the religious so much it drove them mad, and they were venomous at him and wanted to kill Him but could not touch him before His time. Others followed Him only for the fish and the bread. They just wanted the benefits, yet failed to realize that Jesus had set them up to either eat or not eat the bread unto eternal life. This would be Himself. But that is not what they wanted, and they strove amongst themselves because they could not control Him.

John 6:53-64 KJV
Then Jesus said unto them, Verily, verily, I say unto you, Except ye eat the flesh of the Son of man, and drink his blood, ye have no life in you. [54] Whoso eateth my flesh, and drinketh my blood, hath eternal life; and I will raise him up at the last day. [55] For my flesh is meat indeed, and my blood is drink indeed. [56] He that eateth my flesh, and drinketh my blood, dwelleth in me, and I in him. [57] As the living Father hath sent me, and I live by the Father: so he that eateth me, even he shall live by me. [58] This is that bread which came down from heaven: not as your fathers did eat manna, and are dead: he that eateth of this bread shall live for ever. [59] These things said he in the synagogue, as he taught in Capernaum. [60] Many therefore of his disciples, when they had heard this, said, This is an hard saying; who can hear it? [61] When Jesus knew in himself that his disciples murmured at it, he said unto them,

Doth this offend you? [62] What and if ye shall see the Son of man ascend up where he was before? [63] It is the Spirit that quickeneth; the flesh profiteth nothing: the words that I speak unto you, they are Spirit, and they are life. [64] But there are some of you that believe not. For Jesus knew from the beginning who they were that believed not, and who should betray him.

I am not going to break down each section of this (though I'd love to). Yet this discourse between Jesus and the people reveals deep motives of the heart and how it tries to circumvent the rule of Jesus. Jesus went to the very core of the matter without blinking by asking only one question: Does this offend you? He then quickly followed with, «What if you see the son of man ascending up to heaven?» In other words, Go ahead and be offended, and while you're at it, I just might go back up to heaven in front of your eyes! What would you say to that?!

The crux of this conversation reveals why people fail to come to the knowledge of the truth. The Spirit quickens, the flesh has nothing to do with it, and His words are Spirit and life. Jesus already knew that MOST of them didn't believe, and they would even betray him. They were honest when they said, this is a hard saying; who can hear it. Therefore, if you think I'm critical, just realize that Jesus is not looking for followers. He wants disciples. Unless He opens our eyes and allows the Spirit to quicken us, we will not become His disciple, but rather like the masses, we too will leave Him.

The underlying motive is that we only want to believe in God for our own reasons and agenda. They wanted the bread and fish again that Jesus had just fed them. Even so, when we believe only and have no works to show our faith, we merely desire God to give us what we want without giving Him what He requires: our heart. Only then will we discover His Will, and it is HIS Will that must be the WORK we do by FAITH.

Your journey is God›s choice

God made you for Himself, and that means you were assembled perfectly. Everything about you was wired for the journey He has ordained you for. Remember what He told Jeremiah? It is not for us to presume we know why we were born and why God saved us. We must ask Him by drawing near to Him with our whole heart. If we do, He will draw near to us, and we will find Him. We only need to ask one question: are we close enough to Him?

Jeremiah 1:5 AMP
«Before I formed you in the womb, I knew you [and approved of you as My chosen instrument], And before you were born I consecrated you [to Myself as My own]; I have appointed you as a prophet to the nations.»

Examples of Works

James 2:21-26 KJV
Was not Abraham our father justified by works, when he had offered Isaac his son upon the altar? [22] Seest thou how faith wrought with his works,

and by works was faith made perfect? [23] And the scripture was fulfilled which saith, Abraham believed God, and it was imputed unto him for righteousness: and he was called the Friend of God. [24] Ye see then how that by works a man is justified, and not by faith only. [25] Likewise also was not Rahab the harlot justified by works, when she had received the messengers, and had sent them out another way? [26] For as the body without the Spirit is dead, so faith without works is dead also.

Let us not be confused about what the WORK is less we go about to pick and choose it like flowers in a field or food on a menu. Especially those who claim to be apostles but are not. Instead, they are deceitful workers who have transformed themselves into ministers of righteousness, even as Satan did as an angel of light (2 Corinthians 11:13-14).

Notice Abraham›s and Rahab›s works of faith. Their faith was released to do the WORK God told them to do. It was not for their personal gain or to heap it upon their lust (James 4:1-3). It was to carry out the orders of heaven! Unfortunately, today›s modern Church has lost this divine protocol when dealing with God›s Kingdom. Instead, we have presented God as a divine chief waiting for us to tell Him what to cook and for His angels to deliver it to our rooms as we indulge in more spiritual apostasy. We have a fetish for the things of God but would rather not have a desire for just Him.

This is why Abraham was called the Friend of God. Abraham offered up his most cherished hope upon an actual altar. Isaac was bound like a lamb, laid on wood, and Abraham had a real knife raised high with muscles tense as he eyed Isaac's neck. He was in motion bringing that knife down in complete worship until he heard the angel called to him out of heaven!

Genesis 22:11-12 KJV
And the angel of the LORD called unto him out of heaven, and said, Abraham, Abraham: and he said, Here am I. [12] And he said, Lay not thine hand upon the lad, neither do thou any thing unto him: for now I know that thou fearest God, seeing thou hast not withheld thy son, thine only son from me.

We must ask ourselves the ultimate primary question: What and who are we willing to part with to obey God? Do you realize the price Abraham paid to actually be called a Friend of God? It wasn't just a song or worked-up emotion that spilled over into mere words. 25 years of walking with God brought Abraham to this pinnacle of his journey by faith that would ultimately make Abraham the Father of many nations. He had numerous failures and countless trials, but he never lost hope. In fact, He had hope against hope in that he considered God faithful, Who had made the promise (Romans 4:18). It is this WORK that matters to God. It is this WORK that requires faith to fulfill.

Journey By Faith

How can millions of Christian be so deceived into thinking that the work is for things, status, mere daily necessities (which is already included by default for us), or tied to monetary gain? We become aimless in our faith if we have failed to know what God has called us to have faith for. It is that which becomes the WORK in which we validate our faith.

A Prostitute Cuts a Deal

Rahab wasn›t of the children of Israel. She had heard of their God and knew Him to be victorious in battle. With news from the grapevine, she roused enough faith to put her life on the line to hide the spies. I strongly urge you to read right now the entire story in Joshua chapter 2 and then come back to continue.

Joshua 2:9,11 KJV
And she said unto the men, I know that the LORD hath given you the land, and that your terror is fallen upon us, and that all the inhabitants of the land faint because of you. [11] And as soon as we had heard these things, our hearts did melt, neither did there remain any more courage in any man, because of you: for the LORD your God, he is God in heaven above, and in earth beneath.

This portion of the story reveals Rahab›s basis of faith. She declared; I KNOW THAT THE LORD HATH GIVEN YOU THE LAND! Wow! She was a prostitute and a heathen! Yet, she would reject her own nationality and identity on the spot to take hold of the God that she recognized to be in heaven and in the earth beneath! She had seen and heard enough, and her faith was demonstrated by her WORK. She hid the spies, told her own people to chase them over there, and then came back and spelled out the terms of the covenant without hesitation and fear. She wanted in with the God of these Hebrews. Her faith was evident by her placing her life and those of her family on the line! As a result, she was grafted into the family of God that connected her right to Jesus!.

Ultimately, Rahab married Salmon, an Israelite from the tribe of Judah. Her son was Boaz, the husband of Ruth. Joseph, the adoptive father of Jesus, is her direct descendant. ... Rahab was no longer viewed as an unclean prostitute but as one worthy through God›s grace to be part of the lineage Jesus!

Do you need more examples of the WORK of faith that God honors? Read Hebrews 11 starting at verses 7 through 40. So many believers stop at verse 6 and begin to name and claim desires that have nothing to do with God›s Will. False teachers and prophets dare not go past verse 6 because it would destroy their entire false ministry, making people believe they can have what they want and when they want it - if they just believe! It is a demonic birthed from the bowels of a hideous principality that has taken captive millions of souls.

In Jesus› name, you will never have DEAD FAITH AGAIN if you obey the Will of God!

Chapter Eight

Jesus Will Complete the Work

If you think for one second that any portion of your journey is up to you to start and finish, you are grossly misinformed. No explanation can resolve the miraculous ways of God in working salvation Himself in Christ (1 Timothy 3:16), of drawing us to Himself with cords of compassion and love (Hosea 11:4), and of working in us to will and do of His good pleasure (Philippians 2:13).

We have NOT chosen HIM! In fact, when He appeared to us, we were vehemently against Him, wanted nothing to do with Him, and were headlong into ourselves, our agenda, lust, and perversions. We had chosen gods that allowed us to do what we wanted to do and, as a result, were in bondage to fear and trapped in vices of conduct and habits that were destroying us. Nothing we did satisfied. All that we had provided us temporal satisfaction and just became another object no matter how lavish it was.

Journey By Faith

Ephesians 2:1-7 KJV
And you hath he quickened, who were dead in trespasses and sins; [2] Wherein in time past ye walked according to the course of this world, according to the prince of the power of the air, the spirit that now worketh in the children of disobedience: [3] Among whom also we all had our conversation in times past in the lusts of our flesh, fulfilling the desires of the flesh and of the mind; and were by nature the children of wrath, even as others. [4] But God, who is rich in mercy, for his great love wherewith he loved us, [5] Even when we were dead in sins, hath quickened us together with Christ, (by grace ye are saved;) [6] And hath raised us up together, and made us sit together in heavenly places in Christ Jesus: [7] That in the ages to come he might shew the exceeding riches of his grace in his kindness toward us through Christ Jesus.

When we look back, we can see the invisible hand of God, working through the crevices of our lives to cause our path towards eternal damnation to be interrupted by a Savior who would step in our place and become damned for us. He would take our curse (Galatians 3:13), so that the curse would be lifted off our life, and we would be totally new (2 Corinthians 5:17)!

The journey of faith that is before you now was before you before the foundations of the world. Even as you are where you are, it was Jesus who brought you here and will finish what He has started. Let this truth be your confidence. Let this sink deep within your mind, your heart, and your spirit. It becomes a fortress when tempted to think or feel anything contrary to the truth of Jesus is as Lord, and God as your Heavenly Father.

(Philippians 1:6) KJV
"Being confident of this very thing, that he which hath begun a good work in you will perform it until the day of Jesus Christ:"

(Ephesians 2:10) KJV
"For we are his workmanship, created in Christ Jesus unto good works, which God hath before ordained that we should walk in time."

The journey by faith that you are taken
Is on the road He built.
It was built with you in mind
Every twist and turn
Every refreshing spring
Every bird that sings
It was placed there by Him
Tis the reason why you need not take thought for your life
Worry is an absurdity
The spirit of fear and faith cannot coexist
Because Jesus has prearranged everything
You need only believe and take the journey
He's called you to by faith
He has finished it alone by His grace.

Journey By Faith

Be encouraged, my brother and sister, and know that eternity is not too far off. Therefore, resolve in your mind and heart every day to endure. Embrace every ounce of your experience, relish the blessings, and absorb the trials and sufferings, for they have been left for you to partake in His sufferings (1 Peter 4:13). Thus, when His glory is revealed, you will also partake in His glory.

This is your journey. No one can take this voyage but you. You will not draw back to perdition but press to the belief of the saving of your soul! You are of the just, and you embrace the life of faith!

(Hebrews 10:38-39) KJV
"Now the just shall live by faith: but if any man draw back, my soul shall have no pleasure in him. [39] But we are not of them who draw back unto perdition; but of them that believe to the saving of the soul."

He Is Our Confidence

As you fully embrace the truth and power of faith within the ordered Will of God for your life, He will quicken your spirit to know that He will complete the work He has started in you - by faith. From the backdrop of eternity, He already has. When He sealed you with the Holy Spirit of promise, He also completed the work related to that seal (Ephesians 4:30).

This is not a mind game! You will have to fight for your right to experience the journey by faith that God has created you for. You will be opposed, discouraged, and tempted to believe any and everything but the truth that Jesus has completed the work that He created you for - by faith. If you attempt to wait for the natural man to agree with this truth, it never will!

So what do you do?

When you know that you are in harmony with God through clear conscience, obey His directives daily and do what He leads you to do. Then, as you move in faith, He will meet you with direction and directives moment by moment, and if nothing is happening, stand after you have done God's will, and in your standing, He will manifest at His appointed time. Sin not! Worship! In your patience, possess your soul, and you will behold the manifestation of God's will unfolding in His time.

Jesus will complete the work He has started in you!

Steps to Build your faith

The Word of God
Romans 10:17 KJV
So then faith cometh by hearing, and hearing by the word of God.

1 Peter 2:1-2 KJV
Wherefore laying aside all malice, and all guile, and hypocrisies, and envies, and all evil speakings, [2] As newborn babes, desire the sincere milk of the word, that ye may grow thereby:

Hebrews 4:12 KJV
For the word of God is quick, and powerful, and sharper than any twoedged sword, piercing even to the dividing asunder of soul and spirit, and of the joints and marrow, and is a discerner of the thoughts and intents of the heart.

Obedience
Hebrews 11:7 AMP
By faith [with confidence in God and His word] Noah, being warned by God about events not yet seen, in reverence prepared an ark for the salvation of his family. By this [act of obedience] he condemned the world and became an heir of the righteousness which comes by faith.

1 Samuel 15:22 KJV
And Samuel said, Hath the LORD as great delight in burnt offerings and sacrifices, as in obeying the voice of the LORD? Behold, to obey is better than sacrifice, and to hearken than the fat of rams.

Abstain from Sin
1 Peter 2:11 KJV
Dearly beloved, I beseech you as strangers and pilgrims, abstain from fleshly lusts, which war against the soul;

Romans 6:16 KJV
Know ye not, that to whom ye yield yourselves servants to obey, his servants ye are to whom ye obey; whether of sin unto death, or of obedience unto righteousness?

Set your affections on things above

Colossians 3:1-2 KJV
If ye then be risen with Christ, seek those things which are above, where Christ sitteth on the right hand of God. [2] Set your affection on things above, not on things on the earth.

Galatians 5:16 KJV
This I say then, Walk in the Spirit, and ye shall not fulfil the lust of the flesh.

1 Thessalonians 5:22 KJV
Abstain from all appearance of evil.

Don't love the world

1 John 2:15 KJV
Love not the world, neither the things that are in the world. If any man love the world, the love of the Father is not in him.

1 Corinthians 7:31 KJV
And they that use this world, as not abusing it: for the fashion of this world passeth away.

Your whole heart

1 Chronicles 28:9 KJV
And thou, Solomon my son, know thou the God of thy father, and serve him with a perfect heart and with a willing mind: for the LORD searcheth all hearts, and understandeth all the imaginations of the thoughts: if thou seek him, he will be found of thee; but if thou forsake him, he will cast thee off for ever.

Read other books by William Owens

Order at www.throughpeople.com

Faced with untold challenges during his own personal journey, while also confronting his failures, in authentic form, William came to realize that nothing is worth missing the love and the will of God for his life! In this book, William challenges you to Astonish God with your journey of faith no matter what, who, and the countless reasons that would distract you. He confronts the passiveness that has lured many Christians into a "false safe" while warning and encouraging every person he met along the way, as He Astonished God in his journey of faith from Las Vegas, NV to Sweetwater, TX in over 1,000 miles on his bike.

Exposing the problem of bastards in the pulpit is not a choice as servants of God. Rather, it is a mandate, an irrevocable order, a command bearing a weight of responsibility that extends into eternity. It is time for the Body of Christ to boldly identify the difference between one who has been purged from self-interests, political agendas, fear of faces, and hidden sins, even to one who justifies his sins because of grace. In these days of increasing apostasy, we must realize there are sons and then there are bastards…in the pulpit.

The purpose of this book is to point you to the power of God's Word within you. If you do not have God's governing authority working through you to bring about His will in the earth, any hope that you possess will be quickly swept away by this forthcoming conflict. This conflict is manifesting itself increasingly within the natural realm and encroaching upon our society at an alarming rate. War, famine, strange weather patterns, crimes of all kinds, and senseless murder abound. These are signs of the times, and the only effective and relevant place to be is waging a good war! *www.warriorsarise.org*

Naked before God – words that express my heart, is a compilation of poems written during the contemplative times of when William stands before God. During these sacred moments, he unashamedly bares his heart before God and exposes himself to the unfathomable grace, love and understanding that God is so willing to show him. Suddenly – words that express his heart begin to flow! You will be blessed as you grasp the depth, yet simplicity, of these words. While many of these poems are borne out of William's own experience, others are written after reflection upon the lives of both biblical characters and people that have cross his path. *www.nakedbeforeGod.com*

POETIC EXPRESSIONS OF HOPE

A 2-hour Poetry Concert!
watch online at: www.americasaltar.org

THE MERCY & GRACE TOUR

Preaching the gospel in a downtown city in every state of America and visiting churches to pray at the altar for revival!

Evangelist William Owens
972-504-6656
www.americasaltar.org

Listen to my latest sermons

JOURNEY BY FAITH

It is not possible to put in words how much love and thought God put into making you. If that thought shocks you, it shouldn't. The fact that you are even attracted to this statement is evidence that there is a journey inside you waiting for you to discover.

Start Your Journey Today
www.journeybyfaith.net